LET'S-READ-AND-FIND-OUT SCIENCE®

WHERE ARE THE
Night Animals?

MARY ANN FRASER

HarperCollinsPublishers

Special thanks to Robin Dalton at the Queens Wildlife Center
for his time and expert review.

The *Let's-Read-and-Find-Out Science* book series was originated by Dr. Franklyn M. Branley, Astronomer Emeritus and former Chairman of the American Museum–Hayden Planetarium, and was formerly co-edited by him and Dr. Roma Gans, Professor Emeritus of Childhood Education, Teachers College, Columbia University. Text and illustrations for each of the books in the series are checked for accuracy by an expert in the relevant field. For more information about Let's-Read-and-Find-Out Science books, write to HarperCollins Children's Books, 10 East 53rd Street, New York, NY 10022.

HarperCollins®, ■®, and Let's Read-and-Find-Out Science® are trademarks of HarperCollins Publishers Inc.

Library of Congress Cataloging-in-Publication Data
Fraser, Mary Ann.
  Where are the night animals? / by Mary Ann Fraser.
    p.   cm. — (Let's-read-and-find-out science. Stage 1)
  Summary: Describes various nocturnal animals and their nighttime activities, including the opossum, brown bat, and tree frog.
    ISBN 0-06-027717-3. — ISBN 0-06-027718-1 (lib. bdg.). — ISBN 0-06-445176-3 (pbk.)
    1. Nocturnal animals—Juvenile literature.   [1. Nocturnal animals.]   I. Title.   II. Series.
QL755.5.F735   1999   97-34683
591.5'18—dc21   CIP
                                                                                             AC

10

❖

To Mike

4

The summer moon rises over the hill.
A lone coyote howls. It sniffs the air.
Then it begins its nightly hunting route.
With the coyote gone, a skunk scoots out
from its den in a log. Another skunk appears.
The two romp, squeaking and squealing.

5

They don't see the harvest mice
scampering among the fallen branches.
But a watchful barn owl does.
It hoots and goes back to eating
a gopher.

The sound of the owl startles an opossum munching berries. She and her babies duck into the underbrush. Then cautiously she waddles to the pond for a drink.

In the muddy water a raccoon feels around for crayfish and snails. Above, a male tree frog calls to a female tree frog, "*Kreck-ek, kreck-ek.*"

11

A shadow passes over the frog. A little brown bat dips
and dives to snatch moths and mosquitoes from the air.
By dawn it has eaten one quarter of its weight in insects.
The sun rises. The animals retreat to their homes.
The day belongs to others.

13

Some animals are more active during the day. They are called *diurnal*.

Animals that are more active at night are called *nocturnal*. They have adapted to life in the dark. We never see most of these animals. They are hiding during the day when we are awake.

With few people around after sunset,
the coyote feels safe to crawl out of its den.
It yips and howls. From far off, another
coyote answers.

A skunk peeps out from its den and sees
a beetle. It bounds toward the insect.
The skunk's black-and-white fur
blends in with the dark night.

16

Many night creatures are black or gray.
These colors make it hard for their enemies
to see them.

The coyote does not see the skunk.
But its sensitive nose smells it. The coyote
moves too close, and the skunk sprays it
in the face with a foul-smelling, oily fluid.
With a yipe the coyote runs away.

17

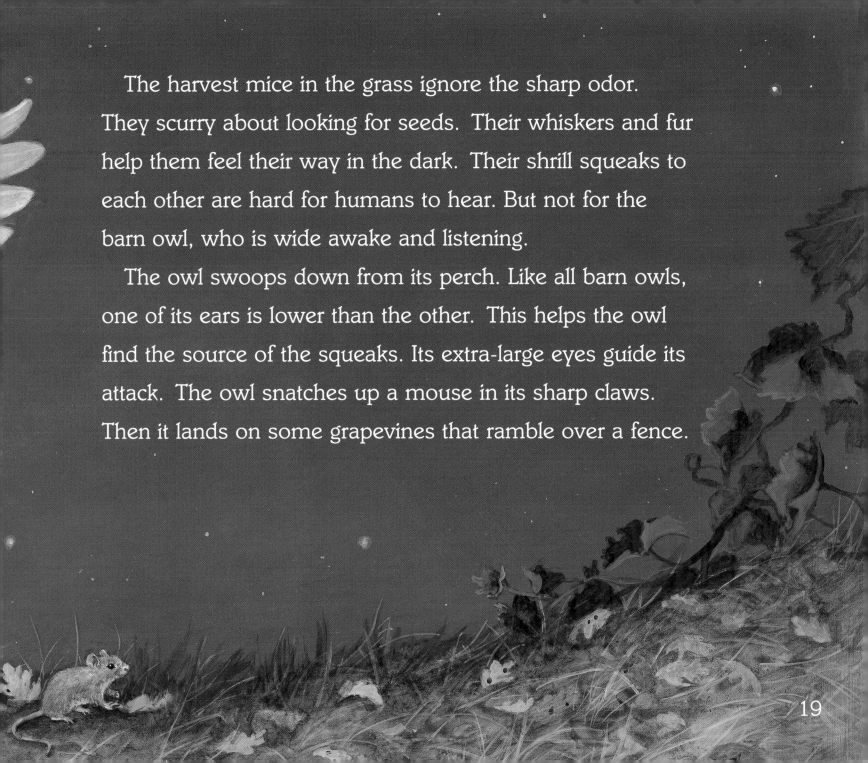

The harvest mice in the grass ignore the sharp odor. They scurry about looking for seeds. Their whiskers and fur help them feel their way in the dark. Their shrill squeaks to each other are hard for humans to hear. But not for the barn owl, who is wide awake and listening.

The owl swoops down from its perch. Like all barn owls, one of its ears is lower than the other. This helps the owl find the source of the squeaks. Its extra-large eyes guide its attack. The owl snatches up a mouse in its sharp claws. Then it lands on some grapevines that ramble over a fence.

The opossum family is feasting on the grapes. Opossums cannot run quickly to escape their enemies, such as coyotes. They must look for food while under the cover of darkness.

An anxious baby opossum sees the owl and tumbles from its mother's back. It lands beside the pond unhurt and climbs back up to safety.

The raccoon comes to the pond every night.
Many nocturnal animals are creatures of habit.
Visiting the same spots each night makes it
easier for them to travel in the dark.

The raccoon snatches a crayfish from the pond.
Then it dashes off with its meal through
some reeds.

The tree frog leaps out of the reeds and lands on an oak tree. This small frog is an amphibian. Amphibians breathe through their lungs and skin. If they were active during the day, the hot sun would dry out their skin, and they would die. Night air is cooler and moister.

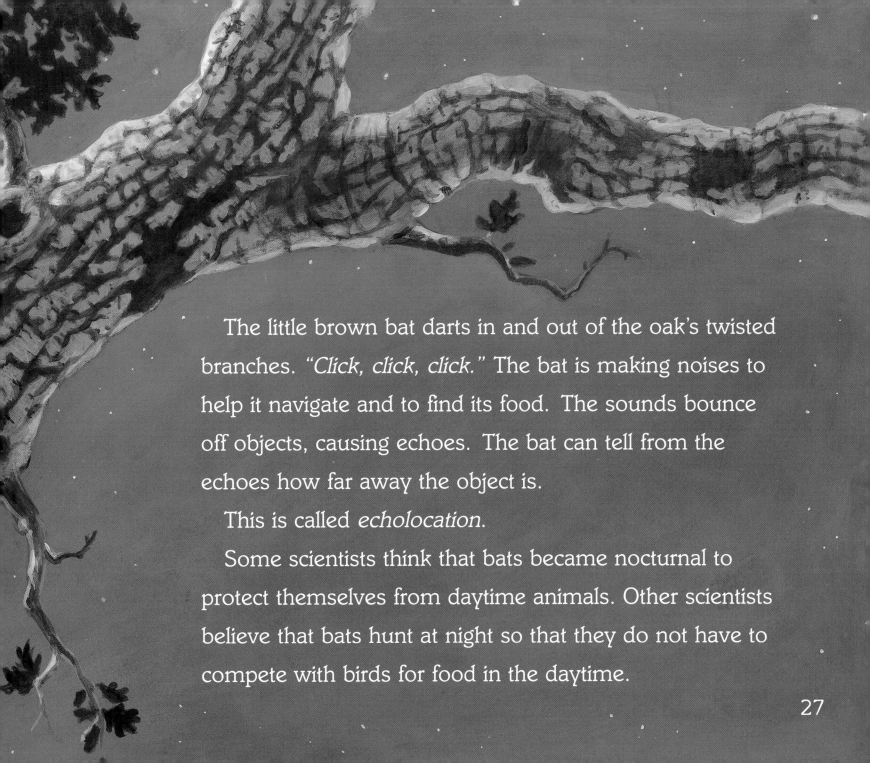

The little brown bat darts in and out of the oak's twisted branches. *"Click, click, click."* The bat is making noises to help it navigate and to find its food. The sounds bounce off objects, causing echoes. The bat can tell from the echoes how far away the object is.

This is called *echolocation*.

Some scientists think that bats became nocturnal to protect themselves from daytime animals. Other scientists believe that bats hunt at night so that they do not have to compete with birds for food in the daytime.

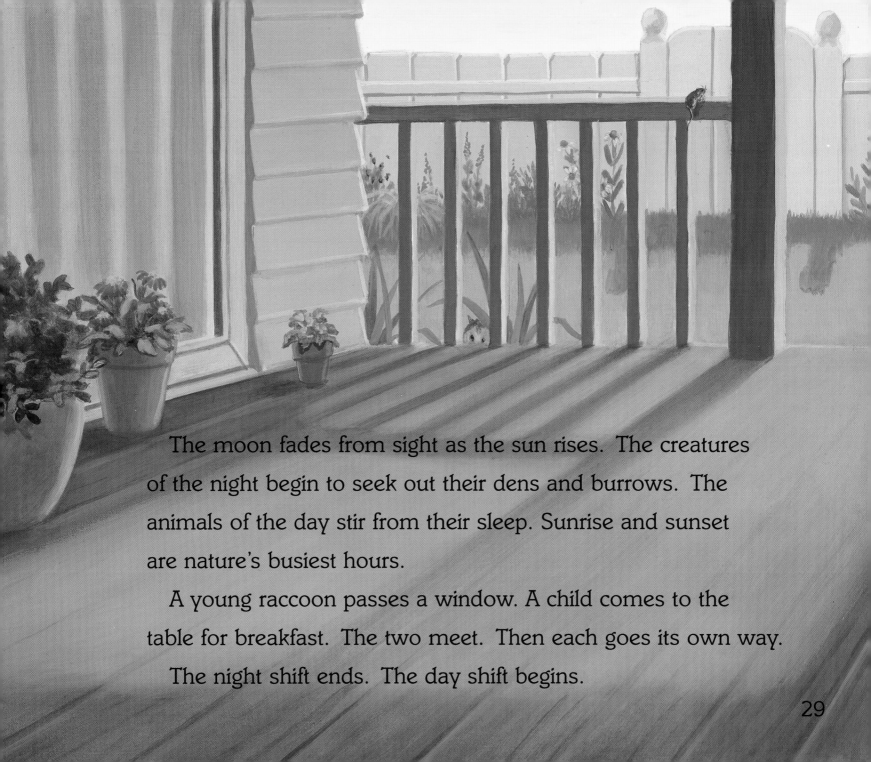

The moon fades from sight as the sun rises. The creatures of the night begin to seek out their dens and burrows. The animals of the day stir from their sleep. Sunrise and sunset are nature's busiest hours.

A young raccoon passes a window. A child comes to the table for breakfast. The two meet. Then each goes its own way. The night shift ends. The day shift begins.

Where do these nocturnal animals go during the day?

Why don't we see nocturnal animals during the day? Where are they hiding? Like people, animals that are active at night don't like to be disturbed when they are sleeping. They look for places that are dark, cool, and safe from their enemies. Some of their hideouts may surprise you.

Coyotes

In the spring coyotes will live in underground dens while raising their pups. At other times they may sleep aboveground, but their homes are always within a few miles of water.

Harvest Mice

These mice live among low-growing plants. They weave amazing ball-like nests out of coarse grasses. The entrance is usually a little round hole on the bottom.

Skunks

Skunks can learn to live almost anywhere. During the day they often hide in hollow logs or other animals' abandoned dens. Around towns they may find a corner under a porch or building in which to rest.

Barn Owls

Despite the name, barn owls also sleep in other types of high places, such as hollow trees or the rafters of abandoned buildings.

Opossums

Opossums will sleep anywhere that is safe from enemies. They shelter in old dens, hollow trees, culverts, and brush piles, and beneath buildings.

Raccoons

Away from the city, raccoons usually spend the day in trees. They will gnaw on the inside of the tree and use the chips for bedding. Sometimes they will sleep in crevices among tree roots, in woodchuck burrows, or simply stretched out on a tree limb. In town raccoons will sleep in drainpipes, sheds, or attics.

Tree Frogs

To keep cool and safe from predators, tree frogs seek shelter in water and wet vegetation. If you look carefully, you might see one crouched under a stone, wedged into a crevice, or tucked into a clump of grass. Near homes they will hide in a drain, near a man-made pond, or even in a well-watered flowerpot.

Bats

Bats like cool, dark places, such as caves, and crevices in trees, rocks, or buildings. They usually sleep in groups and hang by their hind feet.

Where Are the Night Animals?
Find Out More

Play hide-and-seek in the dark.

1. When it's dark outside, turn out the lights in a room in your house, and play hide-and-seek with your friends or family.

2. When it is your turn to hide, be very quiet. Choose the darkest place you can find. You are acting like an opossum or a mouse.

3. When it is your turn to seek, listen for sounds like breathing or shuffling that people make when they hide. Feel around in the shadows. You are acting like an owl or a coyote hunting for food.

4. When you move about, go around the furniture the same way you do when the lights are on. You are acting like a raccoon or a coyote who travels the same route every night.

Look for night animals.

If you live outside a city, you probably live very close to nocturnal animals without ever seeing them. How do you know that they're there?

1. When the ground is soft, go out with a parent in the woods or fields to look for opossum or raccoon tracks.

2. In the evening, go outside and listen. Do you hear owls hooting? If you live near a pond, do you hear frogs calling?

3. Sniff the air. Sometimes you can smell a skunk nearby.

4. Look in the sky. You may see a bat fly overhead.

If you live in a city and you want to see nocturnal animals, visit the zoo closest to your home. They have special rooms where you can see these animals during the day.

Help a mouse build a nest.

A mouse is often in danger at night. Lots of animals want to eat it. It is small and has few defenses. Its nest is a place to hide. By making a mouse house, you can help protect a mouse.

1. You will need five pieces of wood to make a mouse house. Four of the pieces should be 5 inches wide and 6 inches high. One piece should be 5 inches square. Get an adult to help you cut the wood to the right size.

2. Have an adult make a 2-inch-square hole in the middle of one of the 5" x 6" pieces.

3. The four 5" x 6" pieces will form the walls for your mouse house. Glue the 6-inch sides together so that your house is 6 inches high.

4. Glue the 5" x 5" piece on the top to make a roof.

5. Take your mouse house outside and put it near the woods or in a field. Check it periodically to see if a mouse has come to build its nest there.

Developing Library Skills

by
Esther Lakritz

illustrated by Janet Skiles

Cover by Janet Skiles

Copyright © Good Apple, Inc., 1989

ISBN No. 0-86653-481-4

Printing No. 9876

GOOD APPLE, INC.
BOX 299
CARTHAGE, IL 62321-0299

Table of Contents

GA1081

To the Teacher

As an aid for the classroom teacher, *Developing Library Skills* creates situations for students' use of reference materials.

Following the introduction of a reference concept, activities and exercises augment the instruction so that a student feels comfortable with the reference.

From my own experience as an English teacher, I found that once a student is given the clues that characterize a certain reference, he can zero in on any kind of school assignment that would require some research.

The objective at all times is not only knowing how to use the library but where to look for certain information. This means that students will identify the *kinds* of references that will give them the *kinds* of answers to certain *kinds* of questions.

Just flipping through a card catalog, for instance, is of little value if the student is uncertain as to what he's looking for and how he can use it in his assignment, even if he finds it.

Being able to distinguish such clues is essential if students are going to make a beginning through the mass of material that faces them when any kind of research is involved.

GA1081

Chapter I
The Dictionary

The dictionary, as the first reference, has a lot of other information besides definitions. In the same paragraph that defines the word, there are the pronunciation; the foreign language from which it's derived; and the part of speech it represents.

The home dictionary is a good reference for simple questions about definitions, pronunciations, spellings, or usage. The home dictionary is abridged, which means that it limits itself from 130,000 to 150,000 words. The information on these entries will also be abbreviated and/or eliminated.

The school library, however, will have the unabridged dictionaries, which contain over 250,000 entries. There will be many more scientific terms and proper names. The meanings of the words will be more complete. There will be a full historical derivation of a word and in some instances, examples of the usage of words from famous authors.

The unabridged dictionary will have an extensive section on foreign words and phrases. It will also have a gazeteer, a geographic dictionary, which contains the names of towns, villages, rivers, mountains, lakes, and the populations of certain areas.

Clues as to when to use: Searching for definition, usage, pronunciation of words. Unabridged has gazeteer, foreign words, history of words.

GA1081

In Plain Terms

See how quickly you can find the best answers to the following questions. Tell whether you used an abridged or an unabridged dictionary.

1. Who was Nehru? _____

2. What is comechingon? _____

3. Compare the definition of *comb* in an abridged and unabridged dictionary. _____

4. Where does the accent fall in the word *cinnabar*? _____

5. What is the meaning of *corruption of blood* and in what year was it abolished in England? _____

6. What is an adverb for *clandestine*? _____

7. Ernest Hemingway used the word *groove*, meaning "to form a groove," in a description of one of his characters. What were the exact words? _____

8. What do the initials *NTC* signify? _____

9. What is an ascot? _____

10. What is an Osage orange? _____

11. What is the resazurin test? _____

12. What does the abbreviation *misc.* mean? _____

    _____

13. What is the meaning of the Latin phrase *sempervivum*? _____

    _____

14. What is pizzicato?_____

15. Where is the city of Subotica located? _____

16. Define the word *minority.*_____

17. What is a wishbone? _____

18. What is a towzie? _____

19. What do the initials *P.O.W.* mean? _____

20. General Eisenhower coined a new meaning for the word

    stockpile. Can you find the exact quotation? _____

    _____

Dog Days

Using either an abridged or unabridged dictionary, define the following words:

1. bear hug _____

2. pup tent _____

3. horse sense _____

4. fox trot _____

5. eager beaver _____

6. goose pimple _____

7. pig iron _____

8. crocodile tears _____

9. swan song _____

10. cold turkey _____

Abridged Versus Unabridged

Besides the small gazeteer in the back of your own abridged dictionary, make a list of the other types of information you find. Compare this with an unabridged dictionary in your school library.

_____

_____

_____

 GA1081

The Letter of the Law

Tell whether the following words are misspelled. If they are, give the correct spelling, using either an abridged or unabridged dictionary and also tell which dictionary you used.

1. seperate _____

2. embarrassment _____

3. ninty _____

4. foriegn _____

5. judgement _____

6. recieve _____

7. truley _____

8. height _____

9. fourty _____

10. necesarry _____

11. adress _____

12. begining _____

13. believe _____

14. believeable _____

15. carefull _____

16. comming _____

17. mispell _____

18. losing _____

19. neighbor _____

20. aging _____

GA1081

More Than One

Using either an abridged or unabridged dictionary, find the plurals for the following words. Tell which dictionary you used.

1. country _____

2. monkey _____

3. copy _____

4. alley _____

5. chimney _____

6. lady _____

7. friend _____

8. high school _____

9. library _____

10. piece _____

11. sheep _____

12. marksman _____

13. roof _____

14. wolf _____

15. hoof _____

16. cattle _____

17. hero _____

18. boundary _____

19. class _____

20. bough _____

GA1081

At Odds

Define the following, using both abridged and unabridged dictionaries.
Tell which dictionary gave the better definition.

1. Difference between pompano and pompadour. _____

   _____

2. Difference between prevaricate and prevalent. _____

   _____

3. Difference between yoke and yokel. _____

   _____

4. Difference between repertory and repository. _____

   _____

5. Difference between scourge and dirge. _____

   _____

6. Difference between injury and perjury. _____

   _____

7. Difference between catnap and catwalk. _____

   _____

8. Difference between propel and repel. _____

   _____

9. Difference between fuselage and fusillade. _____

   _____

10. Difference between keynote and keystone. _____

    _____

GA1081

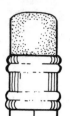

Equal but Unequal

Define a homonym. _____

Tell the difference between the following homonyms and whether you used an abridged or unabridged dictionary to get your answers:

1. calendar and calender _____

2. seer and sere _____

3. vain and vein _____

4. praise and preys _____

5. reign and rein _____

6. sew and sow _____

7. cite and site _____

8. might and mite _____

9. tow and toe _____

10. belle and bell _____

GA1081

Head for the Hills

Alphabetize the following words the way you think you'd find them in the dictionary:

head-on _____

headlong _____

head start _____

headrest _____

heady _____

headstone _____

headstrong _____

headway _____

headset _____

headroom _____

Likes and Unlikes

Define the following:

1. synonym— _____

2. antonym— _____

Using either an abridged or unabridged dictionary, find the synonyms and antonyms of the following:

	Synonym	Antonym
1. constrict	_____	_____
2. decline	_____	_____
3. exaggeration	_____	_____
4. accomplishment	_____	_____
5. hardy	_____	_____
6. foregoing	_____	_____
7. impediment	_____	_____
8. counterfeit	_____	_____
9. permit	_____	_____
10. timid	_____	_____

Did you find you had to use an abridged dictionary for any of the answers? Why? What were the words?

_____

_____

_____

_____

GA1081

Add-Ons

Using either an abridged or unabridged dictionary, define:

1. prefix— _____

2. suffix— _____

Define the following prefixes and suffixes, identifying them as either prefixes or suffixes.

1. pre _____

   _____

2. logy _____

   _____

3. lyze _____

   _____

4. logue _____

   _____

5. semi _____

   _____

6. homo _____

   _____

7. sol _____

   _____

8. uni _____

   _____

9. xylo _____

   _____

10. hydr _____

   _____

Add the above prefixes and suffixes to a word and then define the word.

GA1081

Esoteric Cogitations

Using either an abridged or unabridged dictionary, see if you can figure out what the following words really mean:

1. confidential ocular operative— _____

2. articulating cogitations— _____

3. pusillanimous vagabond— _____

4. indigenous denizen— _____

5. timeous eventuality— _____

6. pervicacious bovine mammal— _____

7. matitutinal refection— _____

8. cephalic habiliment— _____

9. hackney coachman— _____

10. gratuitous comestibles— _____

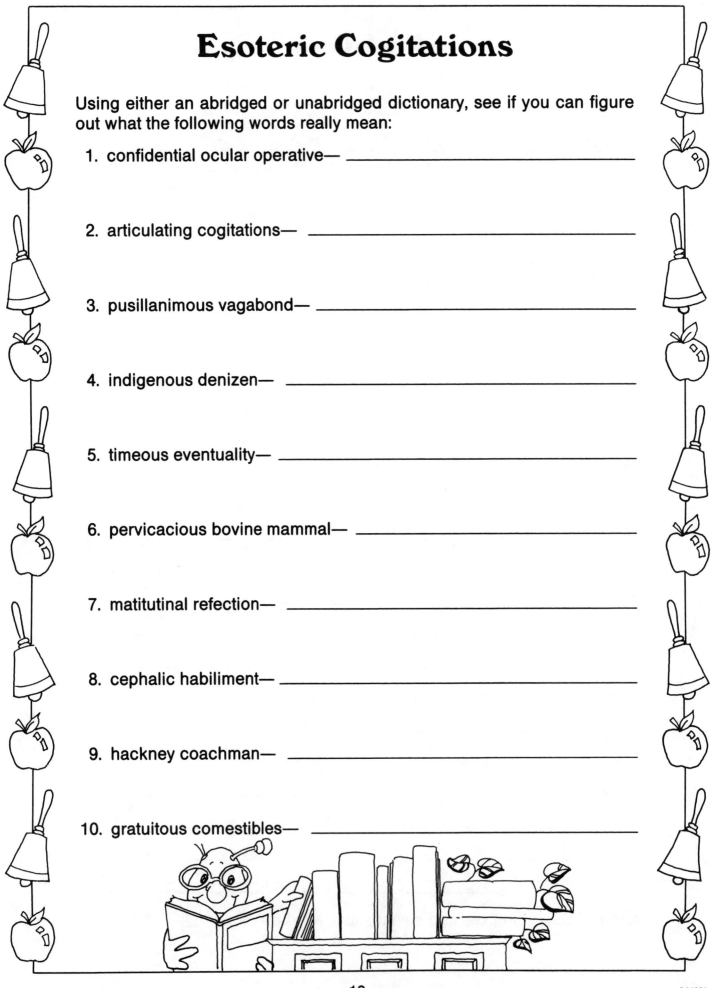

GA1081

Loop-the-Loop Puzzle

Check off each word from the list below. Then circle the word in the puzzle to describe the kind of information the dictionary gives you. Words may be diagonal, backwards, forwards, and may intersect.

```
S   E   R   F   M   B   I   B   L   E   O
P   H   O   N   E   T   I   C   S   W   V
E   R   A   D   Z   W   R   T   U   B   A
L   M   O   Z   L   D   V   B   F   T   S
L   N   L   N   R   P   R   E   F   I   X
I   P   Q   A   O   N   U   P   I   G   R
N   O   U   N   N   U   I   L   X   R   Q
G   M   R   T   C   N   N   U   Y   Z   U
G   O   N   O   S   I   P   R   E   A   O
O   T   O   N   N   G   A   A   T   M   T
B   E   L   Y   R   D   Y   L   H   I   E
A   F   D   M   I   U   N   S   I   O   S
E   R   G   S   Y   N   O   N   Y   M   S
```

spelling	prefix
pronoun	synonyms
noun	antonyms
quotes	plurals
suffix	phonetics

Chapter II
The Encyclopedia

The encyclopedia will give you general information about a person, place, or thing. This work contains facts on almost any topic. A second type of encyclopedia concentrates on one specific branch of knowledge, like science or music.

All subject matter is arranged in alphabetical order. The best way to use an encyclopedia is to start with the index. It will save a lot of time because it will give the number of the volume and pages needed.

There are cross references, too, in the index, which are a guide to additional information.

Under *Rockets* in *Colliers Encyclopedia* (1973 ed.), the cross references look like this:

See also Ballistic missiles; Guided missiles; Rocket engines; Rocket fuels; Rocket propellant; Satellites, Artificial; Space vehicles; and individual rocket weapons or missiles, such as Bazooka, Honest John, Nike-Ajax.

At the end of each article appear the names of the authors with the titles of the books they have written on the same subject. This is a bibliography. Some of these books might be in the school library.

Clues as to when to use: Searching for general information about persons, places, things.

Look It Up

Answer the following questions using any of the encyclopedias in your school library:

1. List cross references under *Mars* you find in the index.

   _____

   _____

2. Where would be the best place to look for the history of musical instruments in the index?

   _____

   _____

3. Give listings for political philosophies in the index.

   _____

   _____

4. How could I find something about Polish cutlery?

   _____

   _____

5. Where would I look to find listings for social welfare?

   _____

   _____

6. I would like some historical material on how the city of London eliminated its smog.

   _____

7. I need some historical information on the Los Angeles freeway system. Can you give me the listings?

   _____

   _____

   _____

8. What listings do you find under *Honeybee*?

   _____

   _____

GA1081

9. What cross references do you find under *Metaphysics*?

_____

_____

_____

10. How is Mexico subdivided in the index?

_____

_____

_____

11. Give a bibliography following an article on the Panama Canal.

_____

_____

_____

12. What "see also" references do you have under *Southeast Asian languages*?

_____

_____

_____

13. List the bibliography following the article on Franklin Delano Roosevelt.

_____

_____

_____

14. How would I go about finding the details surrounding the packed Supreme Court of the Franklin Roosevelt administration?

_____

_____

_____

GA1081

15. I need an account of John Glenn's space flight.

_____

_____

_____

16. How can you find information on the electoral system of France?

_____

_____

_____

17. How are illustrations indicated in the index?

_____

_____

_____

18. How are references in color plates designated in the index?

_____

_____

_____

19. How can you tell the difference between a general heading of a topic and a subhead in the index?

_____

_____

_____

20. If you saw a reference like the following, what would it mean?

Wall decoration: See Mural Painting.

_____

_____

_____

Animal Crackers

Using any of the encyclopedias you have in your school library, see if you can fill in the proper words.

Animal	Zoological Name	Offspring	As a Group
1. elephant			
2. turkey			
3. whale			
4. lion			
5. fox			
6. pig			
7. duck			
8. goose			
9. fish			
10. deer			

What encyclopedia gave you the best answers to the above?

_____

_____

_____

Tell exactly how you went about your search for the answers.

_____

_____

_____

_____

_____

_____

GA1081

Topics, Limited

Using any of the encyclopedias in your school library, find the references to the following topics in the index and list them. Give the name of the encyclopedia you are using.

1. circus acrobats

_____

_____

2. John F. Kennedy

_____

_____

3. hang gliding

_____

_____

4. Eskimos

_____

_____

GA1081

1. Now take another encyclopedia from your library and find the same topics. List the references given in the index, as you did on the previous page. Tell how you think this set of references differs from the first one you looked at, as far as the index is concerned.

_____

_____

_____

_____

_____

_____

2. Which topical index makes you want to read the articles themselves? Why?

_____

_____

_____

GA1081

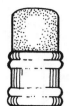

Claim to Fame

Here are some American Colonial occupations. Using any of the encyclopedias in your school library, can you tell exactly what these people did for a living?

1. wigmaker—_____

2. farrier— _____

3. cooper— _____

4. wagoner—_____

5. hatter—_____

6. cutter—_____

7. whitesmith—_____

8. coppersmith— _____

9. glassblower— _____

10. blacksmith—_____

Are any of these occupations done today? Explain._____

_____

_____

Happy Holidays

Using any of your school encyclopedias, can you find the answers to the questions about the following holidays? Give the name of the encyclopedias in which you found your answers.

1. Is Pulaski Memorial Day an American holiday? Where is it celebrated?

_____

_____

_____

2. How did April Fools' Day get its name?

_____

_____

_____

3. Why is Flag Day observed in the U.S.? How is it observed? What is the date of the holiday?

_____

_____

_____

4. What is the difference between Memorial Day, May 30, and Veterans Day, November 11?

_____

_____

_____

How do the abridged and unabridged dictionaries explain these two holidays?

_____

_____

5. For whom was Valentine's Day named and why?

_____

_____

GA1081

6. What exactly is the origin of Halloween?

_____

_____

_____

7. Why do we celebrate Labor Day? What one person started it?

_____

_____

_____

8. What is the vernal equinox and when does it begin?

_____

_____

_____

9. Is Groundhog Day a real national holiday? What's the reason for its place on the calendar?

_____

_____

_____

10. Why do we celebrate Columbus Day on October 12, but Hawaii observes Discoverer's Day on October 10?

_____

_____

_____

Chatter Matter

Select one of the following topics. Read about it in one of your school encyclopedias. List what you find exactly in the index under your topic. Did you find what you read interesting? Write in your own words some of the new facts you learned about your topic. Would you like to read more about it? If not, why not?

1. hurricanes
2. earthquakes
3. chameleon
4. Roy Chapman Andrews
5. Pidgin English
6. trumpeter swan
7. spelunker
8. Anasazi
9. lichens
10. Venus's-flytrap
11. Mont St. Michel
12. ghost town
13. James Bowie

14. Tour de France
15. Abominable Snowman
16. Voyageurs
17. platypus
18. laser
19. eclipse
20. mermaids
21. hydrofoil
22. tornado
23. karate
24. geyser
25. Olmec

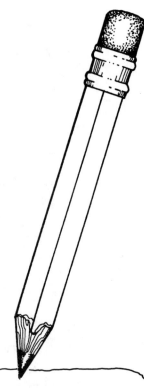

GA1081

More Chatter Matter

Check out your topic, using an unabridged dictionary as a source. Write exactly what you find. List any historical material the dictionary gives. Does this add any new material to the facts you've already read about in an encyclopedia? Would the dictionary information interest you to explore this topic further, if you had not read the encyclopedia? If not, why not? Compare the explanation in the unabridged dictionary to that you find in the abridged.

Cryptogram

The encyclopedia index will help you pinpoint information on the following.
See if you can unscramble the key words.

1. EOPELP

2. CAELPS

3. NETVES

4. MAINALS

5. ALPNTS

6. GNHITS

7. OCSRS REERFNCESE

8. VEDOCISIRES

9. TEVNINIONS

10. ESE OLAS ENERERCFES

11. YORTSHI

12. ARGOHIBYP

13. LIOGPBRAHIBY

14. SEIRNUTOC

15. SPAM

16. TESAD

17. ONOCIMECS

18. GPYHRAEOG

19. RTOGOHPSAPH

20. SHRACT

GA1081

Chapter III
The Card Catalog

The card catalog tells if the library has a certain book and where in the library it will be. The card catalog tells what books contain certain information. The card catalog gives titles of books and names of authors.

Catalog cards are called title cards, author cards, and subject cards.

A title card has the title on

the top line of the card:

> Cool cat
> Bonham, Frank
>   cool cat. Dutton 1971
> 151 p

An author card has the author's

last name on the top line:

> Bonham, Frank
>   Cool cat
> Dutton 1971 151 p

All catalog cards are filed alphabetically by the first word on the card. If the first word, however, begins with an *a, an,* or *the*, the second word is used to place the cards in alphabetical order.

A subject card has the subject listed on the top line:

> 629.14   SPACE
> W65   Wilks, Willard E.
>   The new wilderness; what we know about space
>   McKay 1963   170 p   illus

That number in the upper left-hand corner of the Wilks card is the class number, 600, and indicates that this book deals with an aspect of applied science. Many libraries use a classification system known as the Dewey Decimal System. In the Dewey system, subject matter is divided into ten classifications of general knowledge:

0-99	General Works
100-199	Philosophy
200-299	Religion
300-399	Social Sciences
400-499	Language
500-599	Pure Science
600-699	Applied Science
700-799	Arts and Recreation
800-899	Literature
900-999	History

GA1081

These branches of knowledge are then subdivided into ten additional classifications. The subdivisions are broken down into still another grouping of ten divisions. It is not necessary to memorize the Dewey Decimal System to locate a book in the library.

If the book doesn't belong to a class of knowledge, it won't have a number. Then the book is fiction. All fiction books will be found on the shelf in alphabetical order, according to the author's last name.

Biographies are also a special category. They are in the biography section of the library. There will be a card in the catalog with the letter *B*. Such a card may look something like this:

B Aldrin, Colonel Edwin "Buzz"
AL 23 Return to earth by Col. Edwin "Buzz" Aldrin, Jr., with Wayne Warga N.Y. Random House c.973

The AL 23 will give the location of the book on the shelf in the biography section.

Another special catalog card has an R or an REF as the first part of the number. These are reference books and can be found in the reference section of the library.

Clues as to when to use: Searching for titles, authors, subjects of books in the library.

GA1081

The Cards Will Tell

Now that you are familiar with the way a card catalog functions, see if you can answer the following questions using the card catalog in your school library:

1. What are the titles of books your library has by Joseph Conrad?

   _____

   _____

   _____

2. What "see" and "see also" references do you have under *Holidays*?

   _____

   _____

   _____

3. What "see also" references are listed under *Games*?

   _____

   _____

   _____

4. How would I find something about the gardens of China?

   _____

   _____

   _____

5. How could I find a book whose title I don't know, but whose author is Erle Stanley Gardner?

   _____

   _____

   _____

6. I need some books on U.S. President James Garfield. What listings do you have in your catalog?

   _____

   _____

    GA1081

7. What subject headings do you have for Rome?

_____

_____

_____

8. What "see also" references do you have for your county?

_____

_____

_____

9. What subject headings do you have under *Rock Music*?

_____

_____

_____

10. Give the "see also" references, if any, for the above.

_____

_____

_____

11. What kinds of books does your library have on UFO's?

_____

_____

_____

12. What does the following card tell you?

    301.341   Silver, James Wesley
    Si 3   Mississippi: the closed society
                 Harcourt 1964   250 p illus map

_____

_____

13. Is the following book fiction or nonfiction, and where and how would you find it on the shelf?

_____

_____

A single pebble
Hersey, John Richard
    A single pebble. Knpf   c1956

14. What kind of a catalog card is the above?

_____

15. What kind of a catalog card is the following and where would you expect to find this book?

_____

658.3   Skelton, Dwight
SK2   Fired again; a guide to survival in the corporate
                 foothills.
                 Funk & Wagnalls   1968   164 p

16. I need a book on teenage skin care. How would I find it?

_____

_____

_____

17. What kind of a catalog card is this?

_____

966   SLAVE TRADE
C94   Curtin, Philip D., ed.
                     Africa remembered; narratives by West Africans
                 from the era of the slave trade.
                 Univ. of Wis. Press   c1967

18. What do you find in your card catalog when you look under *Sight,* meaning eyesight?

_____

_____

_____

GA1081

19. What kind of a catalog card is this?

_____

975.3   PRESIDENTS—U.S.
J45   Jensen, Amy LaFollette
            The White House and its thirty-three families.
       New enl. ed. Howard C. Jensen, art editor.
       McGraw 1962   292 p   illus

20. If you saw a number like this on a catalog card, where would you expect to find this book?

_____

       R
      443
      H441
       .3

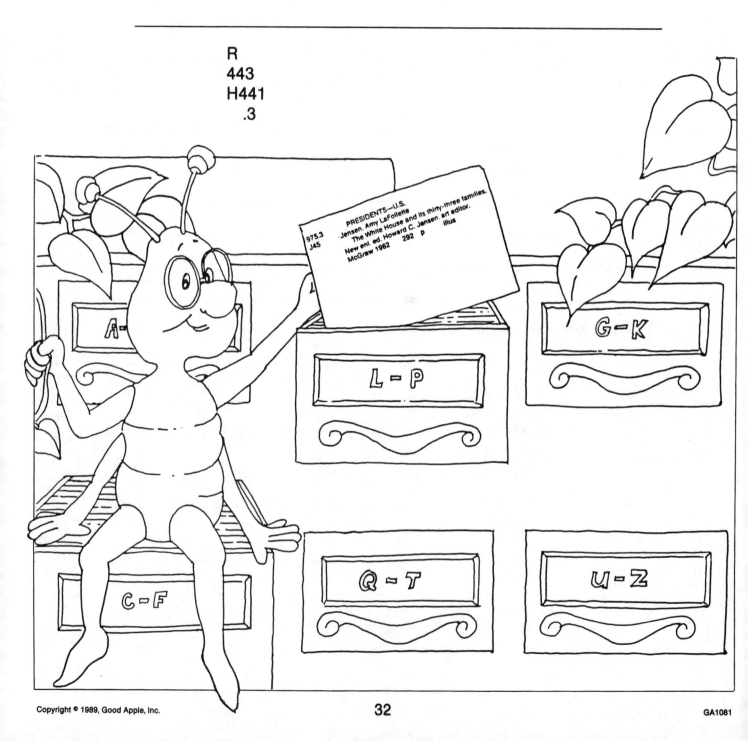

GA1081

Shuffle the Cards

Check out the card catalog for your favorite sport or hobby. Write down the titles of the books and authors on either of these that will be in your school library. Select one of the books from your list and answer the following:

1. Can you tell what the book is about from the title only? If not, why not?

   _____

   _____

   _____

2. Were there any other catalog cards with this author's name? If so, list them.

   _____

   _____

   _____

3. Do you know anything about the author that would tell you whether he or she is an expert on the subject?

   _____

   _____

   _____

4. What does the copyright date tell you? How important is it as it pertains to the subject matter of the book? Does it make the material obsolete in any way?

   _____

   _____

   _____

5. How many pages are in your book? Do you think your book could contain less and still tell you as much about your hobby or sport?

   _____

   _____

   _____

GA1081

A Complete Job

From what you have learned about the order of catalog cards, arrange the following titles the way you think you'd find them in the card catalog.

The Complete Book of Photography
The Complete Book of Cheerleading
The Complete Adventures of the Borrowers
Complete Beginners' Guide to Bowling
Complete Book of Kite Making
Complete Book of Dragons
Complete Book of the Dance
Complete Book of Horses
Complete Book of Fairy Tales and Stories
Complete Book of Indian Crafts and Lore

ABC's of a Book

Below are different titles by the same author. Arrange them as you would expect to find them in the card catalog.

Caudill, Rebecca
  A schoolhouse in the woods
Holt   N.Y.   1949

Caudill, Rebecca
  Happy little family
Holt   N.Y.   1947

Caudill, Rebecca
  A pocketful of cricket
Holt   N.Y.   1964

Caudill, Rebecca
  Did you carry the clay today, Charley?
Holt   N.Y.   1966

Caudill, Rebecca
  A certain shepherd
Holt   N.Y.   1965

Title and Author Hunts

Suggested Games

Divide the class into four relay teams. Make out 3″ x 5″ slips of paper or cards. Each slip will have a nonfiction book title on it from the catalog. Arrange the slips in four piles. The first child from each team steps forward and selects a slip, reads it, goes to the card catalog, finds the book, marks the call number down on the slip and then proceeds to find the book from the stacks. Once he has found it, he returns to the rear of his team, still holding the book. The second child moves forward, selects a slip and follows through as the first, etc. The first team that successfully extracts all the books is the winner. Phase II of this game is the return of the books to the shelves. The first team to complete this job is the winner.

Author Hunt

Relay races set up the same way as above except this time each slip of paper or 3″ x 5″ card contains the title of a book on it. To complete the relay, each student, after selecting a card from the pile, must go to the card catalog, find the author's name, write it on the card and return to the rear of the line, etc.

Title Hunt

Relay races are set up the same way as above except this time each slip of paper or 3″ x 5″ card contains the author's name, and the student must locate the title, write the call number, if there is one, and the title on the slip of paper. First team to complete all titles is the winner.

Paper Chase for Authors

See if you can find the authors of the following books in your card catalog.

1. *The Mysterious Red Tape Gang* by _____

2. *Z for Zachariah* by _____

3. *Swamp Cat* by _____

4. *Cat in the Mirror* by _____

5. *Family at Seven Chimneys* by _____

6. *Nate the Great* by _____

7. *Drake: The Man They Called a Pirate* by _____

8. *A Cup of Courage* by _____

9. *Through a Brief Darkness* by _____

10. *Detectives in Togas* by _____

11. *Ah See and the Spooky House* by _____

12. *Misty of Chincoteague* by _____

13. *The Doctor Who Dared, William Osler* by _____

14. *Franklin D. Roosevelt* by _____

15. *Sacagawea: Bird Girl* by _____

16. *Rascal* by _____

17. *Lassie* by _____

18. *Wee Joseph* by _____

19. *Mara, Daughter of the Nile* by _____

20. *Buffalo Bill* by _____

GA1081

Paper Chase for Titles

Using the card catalog, find the titles for these authors. List all the books if any author has more than one book.

1. M. E. Kerr _____

   _____

2. Jack Schaefer _____

   _____

3. Robert Lawson _____

   _____

4. Arnold Madison _____

   _____

5. Esther Forbes _____

   _____

6. Zilpha Keatley Snyder _____

   _____

7. Madeleine L' Engle _____

   _____

8. Donald Sobol _____

   _____

9. Daniel Mannix _____

   _____

10. Scott Corbett _____

   _____

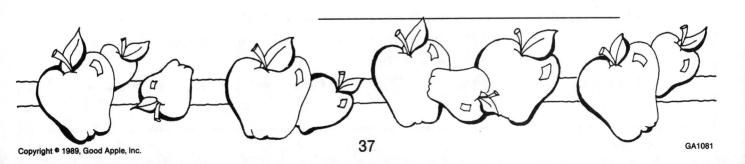

GA1081

Crossword Puzzle

Fill in the spaces from the clues below. Then read 1 Down to find something everybody wants to find.

1. Catalog _____ hold the clues to the books in the library.
2. What does the *c* stand for in *c1966*?
3. What letters on a book stand for reference?
4. A fiction book always tells a _____
5. The name of the classification system.
6. Nonfiction books are placed on the shelf according to their _____.
7. A catalog card that has the name of the book on the top line is (a, an) _____ card.
8. A catalog card that has the writer's name on the top line is (a, an) _____ card.
9. Fiction books are placed on the shelf in alphabetical order according to the author's _____ _____.
10. A cross reference on a catalog card would be written as "see _____."
11. All the catalog cards are in _____ in a cabinet.
12. If you did not know the author's name and you did not know the title of the book, this card would help you.
13. If you found a book with *B* on the spine, what kind of a book is it?

Chapter IV
The Magazine Index

The best general magazine index is the *Reader's Guide to Periodical Literature*. It's an index to more than 180 of the most popular general magazines.

Each magazine article is arranged in alphabetical order, according to subject and author. There is an abbreviation code on the first page, identifying the magazines in the index.

The subject of space flight to Mars had appeared in an article in 1976. The search begins with the *Reader's Guide* index volume for 1976. The entry reads as follows:

> Space flight to Mars
> Aviation W 105:14-17   Ag 16   '76

"Space Flight to Mars" is the title of the article. The article will be found in *Aviation Week and Space Technology*. The number 105 is the volume number of the magazine: 14-17 are the page numbers. Ag 16 '76 is the issue: Aug. 16, 1976.

There are excellent "see" and "see also" references, if the search above had begun with Mars:

> Mars (planet)
>   See also
> Life on Mars
> Space flight to Mars
> Space vehicles—landing systems—Mars
> Atmosphere
> Gravity
> Nomenclature
> See Astronomy—Nomenclatures

Clues as to when to use: Searching for magazine articles on current information.

A Guide for All

1. In the *Reader's Guide* for 1986, what "see" references do you find under *Solar Power*?

   _____

   _____

2. How could I find a *Newsweek* article on SWAT teams? What is the key word in the search?

   _____

   _____

3. Samuel Peck wrote an article about skin care in April 1975. Can you find the complete listing?

   _____

   _____

4. I need current information on reclamation of land in Pennsylvania. Where would I begin to look?

   _____

   _____

5. What "see also" references are there on rock singers? Use any *Reader's Guide* for any year.

   _____

   _____

6. *Seventeen* magazine had an article in 1986 on rock music. Give the complete listing.

   _____

   _____

7. During March 1978-February 1979, there were listings for snowmobile racing. What were they?

   _____

   _____

GA1081

8. Give any notations you find on the Jackson Five in the *Reader's Guide* Vol. 35.

_____

_____

9. I'm trying to locate a copy of a drama, March '75-February '76, entitled "First Monday in October" that appeared in a magazine, but I don't know the playwright's name.

_____

_____

10. Give six subject headings you find under *Finance* in the current *Reader's Guide*.

_____

_____

11. What magazine articles in 1988 are available on figure skating? Give complete listings.

_____

_____

12. Mel Ellis wrote about a one-legged duck in *Today's Health*, January 1975. What was the title of the article?

_____

_____

13. I need an article that was published some time between March '78 and February '79 about legal rights for dolphins. Give complete listing.

_____

_____

14. *Scientific American* published an article in April 1975 about the theory that dinosaurs were warm-blooded. Who was the author of that article?

_____

_____

GA1081

15. There were two excellent articles published about camp counsellors in 1986. Give the complete listings.

_____

_____

16. I want to buy a hand-held calculator for myself but need some expert advice. There was an article published in *Popular Science* in 1986 in the "Shop Talk" column. Give complete listing.

_____

_____

17. List six of the subject headings under *Canada* in the 1988 supplement of *Reader's Guide*.

_____

_____

18. *Sports Illustrated* in April 15, 1974, had an article on Hank Aaron. Give full listing in the index.

_____

_____

19. What "see also" references are given under *Baseball Managers* in the 1986 volume of *Reader's Guide*?

_____

_____

20. You need some current information on careers for women. Tell how you would begin your search and give all the listings you find in the index.

_____

_____

GA1081

The Children's Magazine Guide
Lost Articles

1. How does the *Children's Magazine Guide* differ from the *Reader's Guide to Periodical Literature*? Are the symbols different? Are the magazines different? Give examples.

   _____

   _____

2. Check out the 1984 *Children's Guide* for articles about homemade Christmas gifts. Give complete listings.

   _____

   _____

3. Is there a magazine article about presents for pets in the 1984 *Children's Guide*? Give listings.

   _____

   _____

4. Who was Ansel Adams and in what magazine can I read about him in the 1984 *Children's Guide*? Give complete listing.

   _____

   _____

5. There was a magazine in 1983 which had an article about why moths are attrracted to light. Give listing.

   _____

   _____

6. In what issue in 1985 of *Ranger Rick* and on what pages will I find the article about coconuts by C. Duckworth?

   _____

   _____

7. I read an article about careers in astronomy in October 1984, but now can't find it. Where would I look?

   _____

   _____

GA1081

8. The only listing I've found for computer cars in *Children's Guide* is for November 1984. What's the name of the magazine and what are the page numbers?

_____

9. What magazine in 1985 told why Halley's Comet is so important? Give complete listing.

_____

10. Who wrote an article about the heart in *Jack and Jill* in 1985? In what issue did it appear? Give page numbers.

_____

11. The most current article I found about sleep was published in a magazine in 1986. Give the listing.

_____

12. F. Sunquist wrote an article about crocodiles in 1984. Does the *Children's Guide* have such a listing? If so, give the title of the article, name of the magazine, volume number, issue number, and page number.

_____

_____

13. Are there any listings for crocodiles in the *Reader's Guide* in 1986? List them all.

_____

_____

14. In 1984 Geraldine Ferraro wrote an article for *Glamour* magazine. What was the title?

_____

15. In the 1985 *Reader's Guide* what "see also" references are given under the subject heading *Fear*? Give any article listed under this heading.

_____

_____

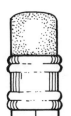

Between the Lines

Another index that is useful is the *Index to Poetry for Children and Young People.* Arranged in alphabetical order, this index lists poets, titles of poems, and the first line of the poem.

Using the *Index*, see if you can find the name of the poem and the poet from only the first line of the poem.

1. "A hideout is a place to play."

   _____

   _____

2. "I'd been away a year, a year."

   _____

   _____

3. "Wynken, Blynken, and Nod one night"

   _____

   _____

4. "I have a little shadow that goes in and out with me."

   _____

   _____

5. "In winter I get up at night"

   _____

   _____

6. "The owl and the pussycat went to sea
   In a beautiful pea green boat."

   _____

   _____

7. "They're changing guard at Buckingham Palace
   Christopher Robin went down with Alice."

   _____

   _____

GA1081

8. I'm looking for a poem about Hiawatha, but I don't know the poet.
I also need a title.

_____

_____

9. Are there any listings about dogs in the *Index*? Give one title of a
poem.

_____

_____

10. Who wrote "Dream Deferred"?

_____

_____

11. Can you find any listings in the *Index* under *Purple*?

_____

_____

12. Did John Greenleaf Whittier even write any poems for children? If
so, list them.

_____

_____

13. Now that you've had a chance to use this *Index*, can you tell how
it differs from the *Reader's Guide*?

_____

_____

14. Edward Lear has quite a few listings in the *Index*. Give six. What
kind of verse did he write?

_____

_____

_____

_____

Square Roots

Reader's Guide and *Children's Guide* give the same kind of information. Can you tell what this is by adding one or more letters below each square for the complete word, circling the missing letters?

I L E T	U S S E	Z N I E

_____ _____ _____

T R I W	J C E T	P G E A

_____ _____ _____

47

GA1081

Chapter V
The Quick Reference Source

The ready reference is short, factual material geared for the instant question that requires an odd bit of information.

How will a search begin for what is the most powerful fuel in the world?

A dictionary won't help; nor will an encyclopedia be of any aid because there is no specific point of reference, no clue to use to find the information. The card catalog will be useless, too; but the *Guinness Book of World Records* won't.

A check of the index will locate the subject. *Guinness* states that "the greatest specific impulse" of any fuel is the "rocket propulsion combination" which "is 447 lbs./f/sec. per lb., produced by liquid fluorine and hydrogen. This compares with a figure of 300 for liquid oxygen and kerosene."

The almanac is another quick reference source. It will supply a single statistic or a brief fact about an event or a country or a person. There will be addresses of agencies and organizations. Almanacs will contain a historical overview of the year past.

Some encyclopedias, like the *World Book* and *Compton's*, issue yearbooks annually. These quick reference sources contain data and statistics for a given year without a long explanation.

Clues as to when to use: Searching for short factual information or a single statistic. When *Guinness* is needed: To find the most or least of a person or thing.

To a Great Degree

Using the *Guinness*, find the answers to the first six questions.

1. Most expensive used cars

   _____

   _____

2. The tallest cathedral spire

   _____

   _____

3. First on both North and South Poles

   _____

   _____

4. Longest horseback ride

   _____

   _____

5. Most valuable painting

   _____

   _____

6. Highest priced orchid

   _____

   _____

7. Taking question 3 above, see if you can find the answer in an encyclopedia. How did you begin your search? What encyclopedia did you use? Also, list your "see" references from the encyclopedia index.

   _____

   _____

GA1081

8. Taking question 5 on the previous page, can you find the answer in one of the almanacs? Tell which almanac you used. What was the key word you used in the index?

_____

_____

9. Taking question 6 on the previous page, find the answer in an encyclopedia. List the "see" references under *Orchid.*

_____

_____

10. *Guinness* gave you the answer to question 5, but where would you find the answer to what was the most expensive painting sold in 1987? Tell in detail how you would begin such a search.

_____

_____

_____

_____

GA1081

Follow the Trail

Using the *Doubleday Children's Almanac* and *Lincoln Library of Essential Information*, name the twelve subject sections in which these two references are divided.

Doubleday Children's Almanac	Lincoln Library of Essential Information
1.	1.
2.	2.
3.	3.
4.	4.
5.	5.
6.	6.
7.	7.
8.	8.
9.	9.
10.	10.
11.	11.
12.	12.

1. How do they compare?

_____

_____

2. How do they differ?

_____

_____

3. Do you think this will make it easier to find quick answers to questions with an index like this? If so, why?

_____

_____

Tell whether you used the *Lincoln* or *Doubleday* to find the answers to the following questions:

1. In what country is Urdu spoken?

_____

2. What wars boosted an interest in toy soldiers?

_____

3. What events make up the Pentathlon? _____

_____

4. Name three motorcycle sports.

_____ _____ _____

5. Why is Emil Zatopek remembered? _____

_____

6. What is reggae? What country does it come from? _____

_____

7. Name the three styles of Greek pillars. _____

_____ _____

8. Who invented the kaleidoscope? _____

9. What is a blind spot? _____

10. How many hairs do we have on our heads? _____

11. What is the tree with the thickest trunk in the world? _____

12. Who were the aborigines? _____

_____

13. What is the most northerly ocean? _____

14. What ocean is the largest and deepest? _____

15. What is the submarine canyon? _____

16. How old is the earth? _____

17. Name three constellations in the southern hemisphere.

_____ _____ _____

18. Name three constellations in the northern hemisphere.

_____ _____ _____

19. What is a fortnight? _____

20. Who was Joseph Stilwell? _____

GA1081

What's My Name?

Using the *Lincoln Library of Essential Information*, can you tell who the real people are behind the following nicknames?

1. Calamity Jane—

   _____

2. Iron Duke—

   _____

3. Father of the Constitution—

   _____

4. Old Hickory—

   _____

5. Blood and Guts—

   _____

6. Sage of Monticello—

   _____

7. Buffalo Bill—

   _____

8. Tippecanoe—

   _____

9. Old Rough and Ready—

   _____

10. Unconditional Surrender—

    _____

11. Taking questions 1, 4 and 7, see if you can find the answers in an encyclopedia. Where did you look first in the index? What were the "see" references? Name of encyclopedia?

    _____

    _____

GA1081

Dig for Clues

Using only the *Lincoln Library of Essential Information,* see how quickly you can find the answers to the following questions:

1. Where in the U.S. is Crater Mound?

   _____

2. Who was the father of Pocahontas?

   _____

3. What sea animal has eight tentacles?

   _____

4. Which was our fiftieth state?

   _____

5. What famous pianist and composer was once Premier of Poland?

   _____

6. What mythical giant held the world on his shoulders?

   _____

7. Where was the first Olympiad held?

   _____

8. What state is called the Bear Flag Republic?

   _____

9. Who was the Colonial American who wrote *Poor Richard's Almanac*?

   _____

10. Who married Pocahontas? _____

11. How many U.S. citizens signed the Declaration of Independence?

    _____

12. In what war did the Battle of San Juan Hill take place?

    _____

13. What famous ship did John Ericson design for the U.S.?

    _____

14. Who was Virgina Dare?

_____

15. In or near what city will you find the largest military hospital in the U.S.?

_____

16. In what city would you find Tulane University? _____

17. What is the national anthem of Great Britain?

_____

18. Why do we remember *U.S.S. Maine*?

_____

19. Why was Vidkun Quisling of Norway called a traitor? How is he remembered today?

_____

20. Where does the Alcan Highway extend?

_____

21. What was the name of Robert E. Lee's horse? _____

22. What is the state flower of Nebraska?

_____

23. The flag of the *Bonhomme Richard* was an American flag. Who made it and for whom?

_____

24. What does the Continental Divide do?

_____

25. Is a sweet potato a vegetable?

_____

Tell whether you find the *Lincoln* index easy or difficult to use. Select one of the above questions and see if you can find the answer in one of the other almanacs in your school library.

_____

 GA1081

Behind the Scenes

Use both *Lincoln* and the *Doubleday* to find who was President when:

1. Pearl Harbor was attacked.

   _____

2. D-Day invasion of Europe took place.

   _____

3. World War I began.

   _____

4. The U.S. bought Alaska.

   _____

5. The Louisiana Purchase was added to the nation.

   _____

6. The Battle of New Orleans was fought.

   _____

7. The Treaty of Versailles was signed.

   _____

8. Indiana became the nineteenth state.

   _____

9. The President was impeached and acquitted.

   _____

10. The Emancipation Proclamation was signed.

    _____

11. Which reference helped you locate the answer faster?

    _____

12. Which reference would you prefer to use and why?

    _____

    _____

GA1081

Strictly Speaking

Using any of the almanacs in your school library, answer the following questions. Tell which of the quick reference sources you used to find answers.

1. What is the major volcano in Antarctica?_____

2. Who was the presiding officer of the U.S. Senate in 1985?

   _____

3. When did Illinois Senator Alan Dixon take office?_____

4. What is the Beaufort wind scale?

   _____

5. Name two major bills passed by the 100th Congress.

   _____

6. Who won the News Photographic Pulitzer Prize in 1945?

   _____

7. What are the names of the opera companies in Texas?

   _____   _____   _____   _____

8. What is the largest commercial bank in the U.S.?

   _____

9. What was the name of the French Premier in 1984?

   _____

10. What is the address of the Procrastinators' Club?

    _____

    How many members do they have? _____

11. Who was the President pro tem of the U.S. Senate in 1987?

    _____

12. What is the motto of the state of Alabama?

    _____

13. What was the worst shipwreck in 1872? _____

14. What is the salary of the President of the U.S.? _____

15. What is the address of the Government Printing Office?

    _____

GA1081

Strays

Use the *Lincoln Library of Essential Information* to answer the following:

1. What does the term *Bank Holiday* mean in the U.S.?

   _____

2. How old do you have to be in Maine to drive a car? _____

3. What is the nickname for the state of Nevada? _____

4. When was vaccination first performed in the U.S.? _____

5. What is the date for the first U.S. transcontinental airmail service?

   _____

6. What does *Aloha Ahiahi* mean in Hawaiian? _____

7. Is there any information about the werewolf in literature? _____

   _____

8. What does the superstition "telling the bees" mean? _____

   _____

9. Why is a barber's pole red and white striped? _____

10. Is there a flower called *wallflower*?_____ What does it

    mean? _____

Famous Utterances

Who uttered these famous words?

1. "The only thing we have to fear is fear itself."_____

2. "Don't fire until you see the whites of their eyes."_____

3. "Don't give up the ship."_____

4. "I have not yet begun to fight."_____

5. "I never met a man I didn't like."_____

6. "Speak softly and carry a big stick."_____

GA1081

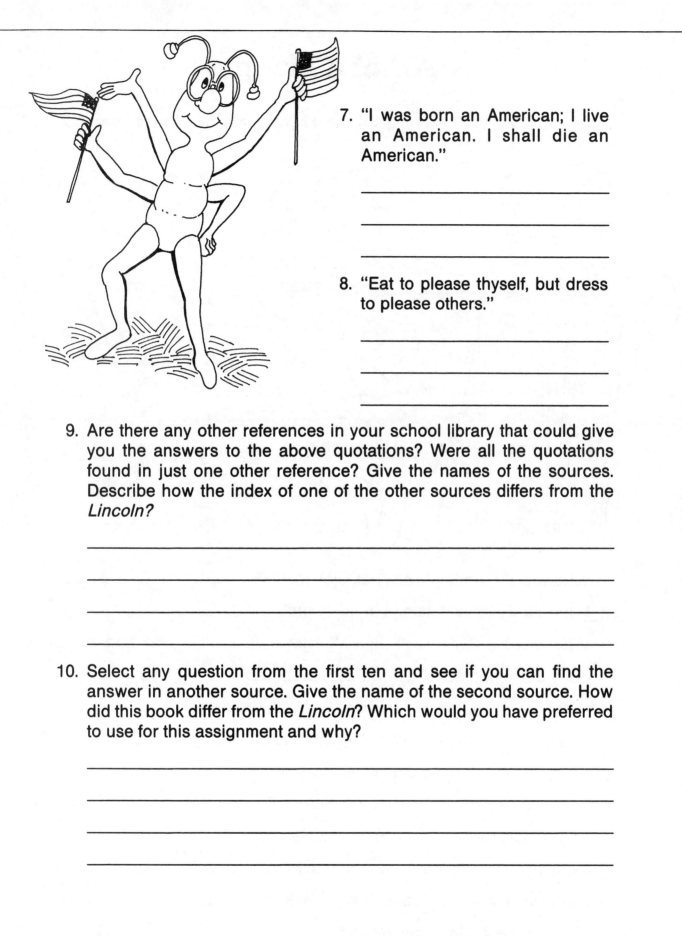

7. "I was born an American; I live an American. I shall die an American."

_____

_____

_____

8. "Eat to please thyself, but dress to please others."

_____

_____

_____

9. Are there any other references in your school library that could give you the answers to the above quotations? Were all the quotations found in just one other reference? Give the names of the sources. Describe how the index of one of the other sources differs from the _Lincoln?_

_____

_____

_____

_____

10. Select any question from the first ten and see if you can find the answer in another source. Give the name of the second source. How did this book differ from the _Lincoln_? Which would you have preferred to use for this assignment and why?

_____

_____

_____

_____

All of a Heap

Tell whether you used *Guinness*, an almanac or an encyclopedia yearbook to find the following answers:

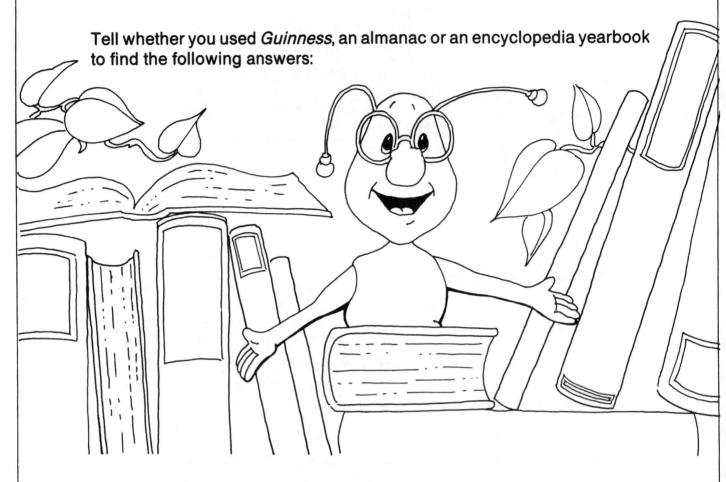

1. Who was the world chess champion in 1966?_____

2. What's the largest diamond in the world? _____

3. Who was the Canadian Prime Minister during 1957-1963 and what party did he represent?_____

4. What's the population of Lumberton, North Carolina?_____

5. What was the longest baseball game? _____

6. Where is St. Edward's University located?_____

7. If you wanted to find some information on Boulder Dam in the almanac, what would be the key word to use in the index? _____

8. Who made the lifetime home run record? _____

9. Who won the Nobel Peace Prize in 1966?_____

10. Where's the world's largest sundial? _____

GA1081

11. What's the busiest airport in the U.S.? _____

12. What is the earliest known mural on man-made walls? _____

13. What is the address of the Antiquarian Society of America?_____

    _____

14. What was the world's worst earthquake?_____

15. What was Hank Aaron's home run record?_____

16. Who earned the Grammy Award for the best record in 1975? What
    was the name of the song? _____

17. What's the official world speed record for the fastest plane? _____

18. What country has the most physicians of any in the world? _____

    _____

19. What was the highest price ever paid for a printed book? What was
    the title of the book?_____

20. Where's the headquarters for The Church of Jesus Christ of Latter
    Day Saints? _____

21. What key word would you use in an almanac if you were searching
    for information about the origin of the name *Montana*? _____

    _____

22. What "see" references does your almanac have under *Money?*_____

    _____

23. If you wanted to find the names of the committees in the U.S. Senate,
    what key word in the almanac index would help?

    _____

24. What is the address of the Boston Symphony Orchestra?

    _____

    _____

25. How would you go about searching for the 1976 luge Olympic gold
    winner in your almanac?

    _____

61

Mix and Match

Can you correctly match the following? Some references might have more than one number.

1. Almanacs _____

2. *Guinness Book of World Records* _____

3. Encyclopedia Yearbook _____

4. *Lincoln Library of Essential Information* _____

1. Divided into twelve general subject headlines, but explanations are brief.

2. Summary of past year's events.

3. Limited information on a recent fact or development.

4. Compendium of data, statistics about events, people, countries.

5. An annual record of data and statistics.

6. A book that gives you the most of everything and everyone.

7. Arranged alphabetically and useful in reading about the political scene of the past year.

8. Best place to get names and addresses of organizations.

GA1081

The Best of All

As you fill out the clues, place the letters in the correctly numbered squares below. The answer is a trivia lover's dream.

1. Shut

$\overline{}\ \overline{}\ \overline{}\ \overline{}\ \overline{}$
22 18 10 8 21

2. Opposite of out

$\overline{}\ \overline{}$
3   4

3. Something to eat

$\overline{}\ \overline{}\ \overline{}\ \overline{}$
14 23 16 25

4. Labor

$\overline{}\ \overline{}\ \overline{}\ \overline{}$
15 13 20 12

5. Lady's garment

$\overline{}\ \overline{}\ \overline{}\ \overline{}\ \overline{}$
19 24 6   7   26

6. Hunter's instrument

$\overline{}\ \overline{}\ \overline{}$
1   2   5

7. Steal

$\overline{}\ \overline{}\ \overline{}$
17 11 9

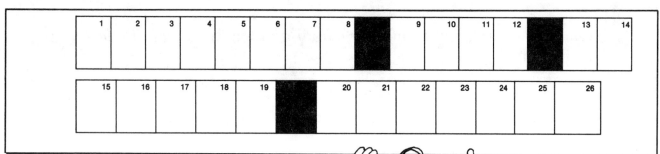

1	2	3	4	5	6	7	8		9	10	11	12		13	14
							■						■		

15	16	17	18	19		20	21	22	23	24	25	26
					■							

Chapter VI
The Vertical File

Another important source of information is the vertical file. The vertical file, sometimes called pamphlet file, includes materials like newspaper clippings, pictures, booklets, and leaflets. There will usually be a number of pamphlets published by the U.S. government.

The government publications are authoritative because they have been written by specialists in government agencies. Much of the material printed has also been the result of years of research, sponsored by the government.

All the materials and publications will be found in special cabinets called vertical files. Everything is filed alphabetically by subject only.

Materials of a vertical file will not be listed in the card catalog. Instead, the library will have a small card file on the top of the vertical file cabinets that indicates exactly what kind of information is being collected.

Vertical files should be used as a source of information. There is no definite rule about what is contained in a file because librarians collect material they think will be of importance to their patrons.

Clues as to when to use: Searching for information on government research or the isolated fact and/or detail characteristic of one's state.

Follow the Tracks

Examine the vertical files in your library and tell the kinds of items you find in them.

GA1081

Single Focus

Select one topic from the vertical file and write in your own words a short paragraph about the subject. Then see if you can find the same material in one of the other reference sources in your school library. Tell what your key word in the index was in using the second source. How did the material in the second source differ from the material in the vertical file?

GA1081

Scrutinize and Analyze

1. List the kinds of pamphlets in the vertical file that are published by your state government. To whom would this information be of value?

_____

_____

_____

_____

_____

2. List the kinds of pamphlets in the vertical file that are published by the federal government. Why do you think the government publishes information like this?

_____

_____

_____

_____

_____

GA1081

Chapter VII
The Gazeteer and the Geographical Dictionary

Sometimes there may be information needed about a city. A map alone just gives the location. But it does not have the correct pronunciation, physical description of the place, or its history. That's when a gazeteer like the *Columbia Lippincott Gazeteer of the World* is convenient.

What's the difference between an atlas and a gazeteer? An atlas is a collection of maps. The gazeteer, without the maps, lists more names, more detailed information about the place, in addition to the usual area and population statistics that most atlases have.

The geographic dictionary, its listings in alphabetical order, does not contain the extensive information as the gazeteer. The *Columbia Lippincott* has 130,000 entries. The *Webster's Geographical Dictionary* has 48,000 entires.

Clues as to when to use: Searching for a good historical and physical description of a place (gazeteer). Searching for a brief description of a place (geographical dictionary).

Here and There

Tell whether you used the *Lippincott* or the *Webster's* to find answers to the following questions:

1. Find the location of the Gulf of Darien.

   _____

2. What is the Enderby Quadrant?

   _____

3. Is there a town in Illinois called Hinsdale? If so, where is it located?

   _____

4. Is Santa Rosa a city in Florida or California? If yes to both, give locations. Then using the gazeteer in your dictionary (can be abridged or unabridged) give the answer you find.

   _____

5. What is Shepherdstown?

   _____

6. What does Umbrella Point mean?

   _____

7. What is the other name of youssoufia?

   _____

8. In what county is the city of Albuquerque, New Mexico, located?

   _____

9. Where is Gettysburg National Military Park? _____
   See if you can find the answer, in addition to a gazeteer, in one other reference source studied so far. Name the source.

   _____

10. Where is Jean Lafitte National Historical Park?

    _____

11. Look up *Whiteside* in *Webster's*. Then compare the answer to one you find in the *Lippincott*. Which do you think is better?

    _____

GA1081

12. Where is the Yellowtail Dam?

_____

13. Use the *Webster's* to find when Kentucky was admitted to the Union. Compare the answer to the explanation given in the *Lippincott*.

_____

_____

_____

14. Use any of the school encyclopedias to find the answer to the above question. Give the name of the encyclopedia used and also list the "see" references you found in the index.

_____

_____

_____

15. Look up the population of New York City in the *Webster's*. Then find the figure in the *Lippincott*. Why do you think the figures are different (if they are). Check out the population figures with an almanac and an encyclopedia yearbook. List your reference sources for each answer. Which figure would you use if you were writing a paper? Why?

_____

_____

_____

A Difference of Opinion

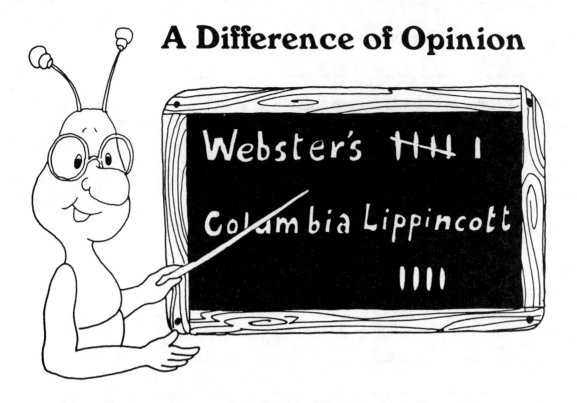

Now that you've used both the *Webster's Geographical Dictionary* and the *Columbia Lippincott*, list what you think are similarities of both references. What are the differences?

_____

_____

_____

_____

_____

_____

Finally, tell which reference source you personally prefer using and why.

_____

_____

_____

_____

_____

_____

GA1081

Trace the Place

The *National Geographic Index*, though not a gazeteer or a geographical dictionary, is about living geography. An index to articles published in the *National Geographic* magazine, it is a valuable resource tool on life in different countries, the people, their customs, their festivals.

I. Suppose you had to give a talk on the Spanish festival, "Running of the Bulls" in Pamplona, Spain. How could you use this index? What would you look up in the *Index*?

_____

_____

_____

Write the references and any cross references or "see also" references you find in the *Index*.

_____

_____

_____

II. Every year the Pennsylvania Dutch hold a fair at Kutztown. What kinds of craftsmen are there to show off their wares? List the references from your search in the *National Geographic Index* you think would be helpful.

_____

_____

_____

_____

_____

III. From everything you have studied so far about reference books, do you think there would be any other sources for the information about the Kutztown Fair? List them, including any and all cross references.

_____

_____

_____

_____

_____

GA1081

True/False

Place a T or F before each statement you think is either true or false.

_____ 1. A gazeteer is like a huge geographical dictionary.

_____ 2. The geographical dictionary is different because it lists the airports of the world, along with highways and railroads.

_____ 3. In order to understand a gazeteer, you should know the difference between latitude and longitude.

_____ 4. Before you can use a geographical dictionary, you must first figure out where north is.

_____ 5. The *Columbia Lippincott* gives additional data like the industry of a place and its natural resources.

_____ 6. The average gazeteer has even more maps than the average atlas.

_____ 7. The *National Geographic Index* is like an encyclopedia index, listing topics according to subject, title, author.

_____ 8. *Webster's Geographical Dictionary* has no index to help locate names.

_____ 9. A dictionary gazeteer gives a brief description of the names of cities, islands, lakes, rivers, and countries.

_____10. Anyone who works on a gazette is known as a gazeteer.

_____11. Both the *Lippincott* and the *Webster's* are dictionaries because they are arranged in alphabetical order.

_____12. The gazeteer in an abridged dictionary contains the same quantity of information as *Webster's*.

_____13. The unabridged dictionary has more entries on locations of places than the *Lippincott*.

_____14. The *National Geographic Index* features people and customs throughout the world.

Wheel of Reference

Answer the clues by placing the words on the spokes of the Wheel of Reference and discover more information the Gazeteer contains.

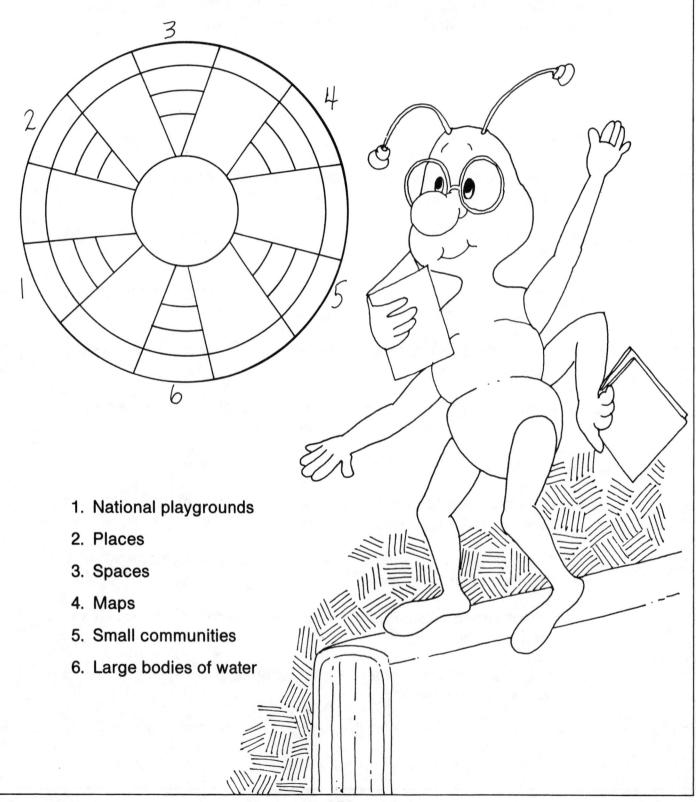

1. National playgrounds
2. Places
3. Spaces
4. Maps
5. Small communities
6. Large bodies of water

74

Chapter VIII
Biographies

There are collective biographies, autobiographies, and biographies.

The collective biography is a book containing several biographical sketches of prominent people.

The autobiography is the story of a life about the author by the author himself.

The biography is the story of a life written by one other than the subject of the biography.

Encyclopedias and yearbooks include biographical sketches on the more important men and women and so do almanacs.

Who's Who in America is a collective biography which gives short biographical facts about well-known living Americans.

Webster's Biographical Dictionary lists 40,000 names for all periods of time and all countries, not just Americans.

The *Dictionary of American Biography* has longer entries about Americans who are no longer alive. The *DAB* is more interested in those who made a contribution to the American way of life.

Clues as to when to use: Searching for short sketches of living Americans (*Who's Who*). Searching for extensive accounts of past Americans (*DAB*). Searching for universal sketches of people everywhere, past and present (*Webster's*).

GA1081

People Pleasers

1. You need a quick sketch of a person who's going to appear at your assembly program and you have to introduce him. What reference would you use and why?

   _____

   _____

   _____

   _____

2. Compare the listing in the back of your dictionary of Louisa May Alcott to the *Dictionary of American Biography*. How does this differ from the version you might find in *Something About the Author*, another collective biography? Compare the material to a sketch about the subject in one of your school encyclopedias. Were there any cross references in the encyclopedia? If so, list them.

   _____

   _____

   _____

   _____

3. Compare information about Clara Barton in the *Dictionary of American Biography*, any encyclopedia, and the *Lincoln Library of Essential Information*.

   a. Which is the sketchiest?

   _____

   _____

   b. Which entry wants you to read on and find out more information?

   _____

   _____

   c. Check out the card catalog for additional entries and list them, including all cross references.

   _____

   _____

4. Where can you find a biographical sketch of Michael Jackson?

_____

5. Is there any current information on Cory Aquino of the Philippines?

_____

6. Check out the *Dictionary of American Biography* for a biographical sketch of Theodore Roosevelt. Compare that to *Webster's Biographical Dictionary* and any encyclopedia you have in your school library. Which one is better and why? What are the references in the card catalog?

_____

_____

_____

7. What was the real name of Lewis Carroll? What is his famous story? Why didn't he write it under his own name? Use either an encyclopedia or any collective biography in your school library to find the answer. Give the reference book you used.

_____

_____

_____

8. What do you think is the difference between a nonfiction and a fiction biography?

_____

_____

9. What two catalog cards would tell you the book was a fictional biography?

_____

_____

10. How would a fictional biography be placed on the library shelf?

_____

_____

GA1081

Ladies, First

Using the *Dictionary of American Biography*, find the names of the wives of the following Presidents:

1. Calvin Coolidge   _____

2. John Adams   _____

3. James Polk   _____

4. Zachary Taylor   _____

5. Abraham Lincoln   _____

6. Thomas Jefferson   _____

7. Ulysses S. Grant   _____

8. Grover Cleveland   _____

9. James Garfield   _____

10. William McKinley   _____

11. James Buchanan   _____

12. William Howard Taft   _____

13. James Madison   _____

14. Andrew Jackson   _____

15. Theodore Roosevelt   _____

16. Martin Van Buren   _____

17. James Monroe   _____

18. John Quincy Adams   _____

19. Andrew Johnson   _____

20. William Henry Harrison   _____

GA1081

First with the Most

Using the *Dictionary of American Biography*, give the occupation for each and tell why he/she was famous.

1. Lewis Waterman   _____

2. Linus Yale   _____

3. W. A Roebling   _____

4. Ann Dudley Bradstreet   _____

5. Josiah Foster Flagg   _____

6. John Wanamaker   _____

7. Edward Stratemeyer   _____

8. Elizabeth Blackwell   _____

9. Crispus Attucks   _____

10. Charles Sherwood Stratton   _____

11. Edgar Allan Poe   _____

****

12. What is the nickname of Elizabeth Cochrane Seaman? What did she do to make her famous?

_____

_____

13. Mary Ludwig Hays McCauley will also go down in history by another name. What is it and how did she get it?

_____

_____

GA1081

14. What was Henry Lee's nickname and to whom was he related?

_____

_____

15. Edward Everett was the candidate for the U.S. presidency from what party? What was the year of the campaign? Who was the presidential candidate on this ticket?

_____

_____

16. Give all listings in your card catalog under Edgar Allan Poe.

_____

_____

17. What books do you have in your school library about Nellie Bly? List both fiction and nonfiction.

_____

_____

18. Compare the account of Crispus Attucks in any school encyclopedia with that of the *DAB*. Give listings from the encyclopedia index about Crispus Attucks.

_____

_____

19. Are there listings for Molly Pitcher in your card catalog? Note them below.

_____

_____

20. From all the information given on Nellie Bly, Crispus Attucks, and Molly Pitcher, whom would you like to read more about? Why?

_____

_____

GA1081

Catch a Rising Star

Using *Who's Who in America*, find out the occupation of each of the following:

1. Johnny Cash _____

2. Jacques Cousteau _____

3. Sarah Caldwell _____

4. Ellen Burstyn _____

5. Charles Yeager _____

6. What position did Robert Clifton Weaver hold in the cabinet of President Lyndon Johnson? _____

7. Lucille Ball _____

8. What position did Dean Rusk hold in President Lyndon Johnson's cabinet? _____

9. David Letterman _____

10. Jackson Pollock _____

11. Aaron Copland _____

12. What position in President Jimmy Carter's administration did Clifford Leopold Alexander, Jr., hold? _____

13. C. Douglas Dillon was the Secretary of the Treasury during what years?

14. In the *Reader's Guide* issue of August 1987, there was a listing about Jacques Cousteau. Give the magazine, date of magazine, pages, and title of article. _____

_____

_____

GA1081

15. Check out the card catalog for any books by and about Jacques Cousteau and list them.

_____

_____

_____

16. What is Ellen Burstyn's real name?

_____

17. Name two musical works for which Aaron Copland is famous.

_____

_____

18. Are there books in your library about Johnny Cash? If so, list them.

_____

_____

19. Is there a listing in your card catalog for the biography of Charles Yeager? Give title and author.

_____

_____

Are there any books about test pilots in your school library? List them.

_____

_____

20. In November 1987, there was an article in which Charles Yeager talks about "breaking the sound barrier." Give the name of the magazine, volume, and pages, as found in the *Reader's Guide.*

_____

_____

_____

21. *Newsweek* magazine also had an article about Yeager, on July 27, 1987. What was the title of the article?

_____

GA1081

Civil Servants

The following held an office in the government, either as vice president, cabinet officer, Speaker of the House, or governor of a state. Using the *Dictionary of American Biography*, find the proper office and name the presidential administration, if a federal office.

1. William Seward _____

2. Champ Clark
   What four states supported him for President in the preconvention campaign of 1912? _____
   _____
   _____

3. Garrett Hobart _____

4. Charles Fairbanks _____

5. Salmon P. Chase _____

6. Oliver Ellsworth _____

7. John Marshall _____

8. Alexander Hamilton _____

9. John Jay _____

10. Robert LaFollette _____

****

The following can be found in *Who's Who in America*. List the government positions held.

11. William P. Rogers _____

12. George Shultz _____

13. Gerald R. Ford _____

14. Melvin Laird _____

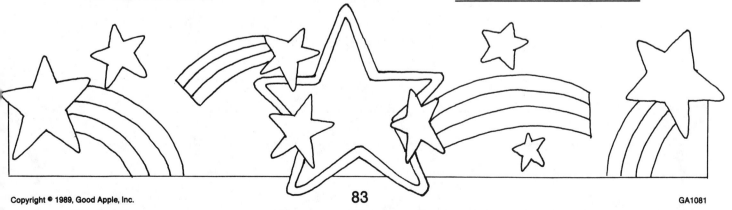

GA1081

15. Check out your card catalog for any books on Salmon P. Chase and list them.

_____

_____

_____

16. What was Seward's Folly and how did it get that name?

_____

_____

_____

17. Does your card catalog have anything under *Alexander Hamilton*? List all the references.

_____

_____

_____

18. Check the card catalog to see if your library has any books about Gerald Ford and write them below.

_____

_____

_____

19. Using any school encyclopedia, list all references in the index that pertain to John Marshall. Name the encyclopedia.

_____

_____

_____

20. The name of Sam Bass appears in the *Dictionary of American Biography*. Why do you think he would rate a listing? Do any of your school encyclopedias have an account of Sam Bass? If so, does this version differ from the one in the *DAB*? Explain.

_____

_____

_____

GA1081

Thumbnail Sketches

What are the occupations of the following and what is their claim to fame, as listed in *Who's Who in America*?

1. Edwin Land _____

2. Jonas Salk _____

3. James Van Allen _____

4. Jerome Karle _____

5. Herbert Hauptman _____

****

How does *Who's Who* describe these?

6. Ralph Nader _____
   What was the name of the book he wrote in 1965 that brought him fame?

   _____

7. Irving Berlin _____

   How many songs, altogether, did he write? _____

8. James Michener _____

   A book of his published in 1985 was entitled _____

   _____

9. Walter Cronkite _____

10. Mortimer Adler _____

11. In the February 1988 issue of *Reader's Guide*, there is an interview of Walter Cronkite listed. Give the magazine, date, pages, and author of article.

    _____

12. In November 1987, I. Wolfman wrote an article about Ralph Nader. Give the complete listing in *Reader's Guide*.

    _____

13. W. Greider interviewed Ralph Nader, November 1987. In what magazine did it appear?

    _____

GA1081

Rebus Twister

Can you solve this puzzle and discover the name of an important reference source?

CET +  + 👁 − DYE + 🕐 − ❤

+ T + 5 − F

2 + O + ▦ + YOU − OU

_____
_____
_____

−W

86

GA1081

Find the Resource

Now that you've learned how to find most answers to questions, you should be ready to answer the following and tell where would be the best place to find the answers.

1. Where can I find a definition and picture of a shillelagh?

   _____

2. What is the historical derivation of the word *library*?

   _____

3. Where can I find information about Peter Mark Roget?

   _____

4. I need some current information about American technical assistance to Iran.

   _____

5. What is the status of migrant labor in your state?

   _____

6. What's the greatest altitude ever reached by an aircraft?

   _____

7. Where are your state's more popular camping sites?

   _____

8. I have to give a short talk to the class on the habits and life cycle of the Brachiopoda.

   _____

9. I have to give a book review on Dorothy Canfield's novella *Bonfire*. Where can I find it?

   _____

10. I have to give a speech for our spring assembly program on kite flying, and I don't know how many books our library even has on the subject.

   _____

11. I'm supposed to talk for five minutes on Edward Braddock, the British commander-in-chief in North America during the French and Indian War.

_____

12. My social science teacher asked me to find the different kinds of churches in my state.

_____

13. What is a crystal spectrometer? Where should I begin to look for such an answer?

_____

14. My friend and I disagree on what's the oldest planet in the universe. How can we settle the argument?

_____

15. If you saw a notation like this on a catalog card, what would it mean to you?

    Skis and Skiing
        See also pamphlet file

_____

16. Besides *Little Women*, how can I find what other books by Louisa M. Alcott my library has?

_____

17. What is the correct spelling of the word *embarass* ?

_____

18. What is the correct pronunciation of *incognito*?

_____

19. How can I find the story of *Ali Baba* in my library?

_____

20. I need a bibliography on computers.

_____

21. I'm giving a talk on food additives and need current information.

_____

22. How can I find the adverb for the word *prig*?

_____

23. What foreign language does the word *orchestre* come from?

_____

24. Where's the best place to find where Tadzhik is located?

_____

25. If I wanted to get some information on why the French Canadians in Quebec want to separate from the rest of Canada, where would I look?

_____

26. What is a doggie?

_____

27. Where can I get a copy of "The Tell-Tale Heart" by Edgar Allan Poe?

_____

28. What is the largest ocean in the world?

_____

29. What was the first permanent settlement in America?

_____

30. Where can I find out about ham radio?

_____

31. Where did the Incas live?

_____

32. Who wrote *Adventures of Tom Sawyer*?

_____

33. What was the *Titanic* and what happened to it?

_____

34. Where can I learn about the seat belt law in my state?

_____

35. How did California get its name?

_____

36. How long is a regulation football field? _____

37. Does the Mississippi River flow north? _____

38. What issue in *Cricket Magazine* is the article about vampires?

_____

39. Where can I find a story about Santa's alphabet?

_____

40. What's the title of the poem whose first line is "My poor old bones—I've only two"?

_____

41. In what state are the Green Mountains? _____

42. Where is the source of the Ohio River? _____

43. Who was President when the Lewis and Clark Expedition took place?

_____

44. What was the name of Robert Fulton's steamship? _____

45. What's the difference between an antonym and a synonym?

_____

46. Where could I get up-to-the-minute information about the energy situation in this country?

_____

47. Where can I get statistics on auto accidents in my state?

_____

48. I have to give a report on the history of the clarinet. Where's the best place to begin my research?

_____

49. My class is planning a field trip to Washington, D.C. I need names and addresses of museums to visit.

_____

50. Where in the library can I find a science encyclopedia?

_____

 GA1081

Answer Key

Pages 2-3 In Plain Terms
1. Indian Prime Minister (abridged)
2. An extinct language of Argentina (only answer in *Webster's 3rd New International*)
3. Unabridged has 22 different definitions.
   Abridged—a toothed instrument used especially for adjusting, cleaning, confining hair
4. First syllable (abridged)
5. English law: the impurity before law that results from attainder and disqualifies the attainted person from inheriting, retaining, or bequeathing lands or interests in lands, abolished in 1870 (unabridged)
6. Clandestinely (abridged)
7. "Eyes with faint white wrinkles at the corners that grooved merrily when he smiled" (*Webster's 3rd New International*)
8. Negative temperature coefficient (*Webster's 3rd New International*)
9. Broad neck scarf (abridged)
10. Ornamental American tree of mulberry family with shiny ovate leaves and hard bright orangewood (abridged)
11. Used as an oxidation reduction indicator in the resazurin test for bacteria (unabridged)
12. Miscellaneous
13. Any of various succulent plants belonging to the genus sempervivum of the stonecrop family (unabridged)
14. A note or passage played by plucking strings (abridged)
15. Yugoslavia
16. The smaller in number of two groups (abridged)
17. Superstition when two persons pull it apart, the one getting the longer fragment will have his wish granted. (abridged)
18. Scottish variation of tousy (unabridged)
19. Prisoner of War (abridged)
20. "Strengthen its civil defense stockpile of medical . . . supplies." (*Webster's 3rd New International*)

Page 4 Dog Days
1. A rough tight embrace
2. A wedge-shaped shelter tent usually without flooring or sidewalls
3. Common sense
4. A dance
5. One who is extremely zealous in performing his assigned duties and is volunteering for more
6. Gooseflesh
7. Crude iron that is the direct product of the blast furnace and is refined to produce steel
8. False tears; hypocritical sorrow
9. A farewell appearance or final act
10. Abrupt complete cessation of the use of an addictive drug

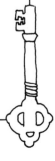

GA1081

Page 4 Abridged Versus Unabridged

Abridged (*Webster's New Collegiate*): List of colleges and universities; biographical names, foreign words and phrases; geographical names; signs and symbols in astronomy, biology, business, chemistry, flowchart, math, medicine, miscellaneous, physics, reference marks, stamps and stamp collecting, weather. Also has handbook of style: punctuation, plurals, capitalization. Instruction on how to write footnotes, forms of address; style in business correspondence.

Random House Dictionary of the English Language Second Edition 1987: In addition to the contents of the abridged, as above, the *Random House* has concise French dictionary, concise Spanish dictionary, concise Italian dictionary, concise German dictionary; words commonly confused; words commonly misspelled; atlas of world.

Page 5 The Letter of the Law

1. yes—separate	6. yes—receive	11. yes—address	16. yes—coming
2. no	7. yes—truly	12. yes—beginning	17. yes—misspell
3. yes—ninety	8. no	13. no	18. no
4. yes—foreign	9. yes—forty	14. yes—believable	19. no
5. no—judgment or judgement	10. yes—necessary	15. yes—careful	20. no

Page 6 More Than One (used an abridged)

1. countries	6. ladies	11. sheep	16. cattle
2. monkeys	7. friends	12. marksmen	17. heroes
3. copies	8. high schools	13. roofs	18. boundaries
4. alleys	9. libraries	14. wolves	19. classes
5. chimneys	10. pieces	15. hoofs or hooves	20. boughs

Page 7 At Odds

1. A marine percoid fish of South Atlantic and Gulf coasts (abridged)
   A deep-bodied food fish (unabridged)
   A woman's style of hairdressing in which hair is combed into a high mound in front to stand erect (abridged)
   An arrangement of man's hair in which it is brushed up high from forehead. Woman's hair—raised over forehead in a roll. Named after Marquise de Pompadour. (unabridged)
2. To deviate from truth (abridged)
   To speak falsely or deliberately misstate (unabridged)
   Generally or widely accepted (abridged)
   Of wide occurrence (unabridged)
3. Wooden bar or frame by which two draft animals are joined at heads and necks (abridged)
   A device for joining together a pair of draft animals, like oxen (unabridged)
   An inhabitant of a rural area (abridged)
   A rustic, country bumpkin (unabridged)
4. A theater in which several different plays are presented in a season by a resident company (abridged)
   A type of theatrical presentation in which a company presents several works regularly or in alternate sequence in one season (unabridged)
   A place where something is stored or deposited (abridged)
   A receptacle or place where things are stored, deposited, offered for sale (unabridged)
5. A cause of widespread or great affliction (abridged)

GA1081

A cause of affliction or calamity: disease, famine are scourges of humanity (unabridged)

A slow, solemn, mournful piece of music (abridged)

A funeral song (unabridged)

6. Hurt or damage (abridged)

Harm or language that is done or sustained (unabridged)

False swearing (abridged)

The wilful giving of false testimony under oath before a tribunal upon a point of material to a legal inquiry (unabridged)

7. Short, light nap (abridged)

A short, light doze (unabridged)

A narrow walkway, as along a bridge (abridged)

A narrow walkway, especially one high above the surrounding area used to provide access as over the stage in a theater (unabridged)

8. To drive forward and onward (abridged)

To drive, or cause to move forward or onward (unabridged)

To drive away, turn away (abridged)

To drive or force back an assailant or invader (unabridged)

9. Central body portion of airplane (abridged)

The complete central structure in which the wing, tail surfaces, and engines are attached on an airplane (unabridged)

A number of shots fired simultaneously or in rapid succession (abridged)

A general discharge of firearms or outpouring of anything; a fusillade of questions (unabridged)

10. The fundamental and central fact, idea, or mood (abridged)

The main idea or central principle of a speech, program, thought, action. The policy line to be followed as by a party in a political campaign that is set forth authoritatively in advance by an address or other formal announcement (unabridged)

The wedge-shaped piece at the crown of an arch that locks other pieces in place (abridged)

The wedge-shaped piece of the summit of an arch, regarded as holding the other pieces in place. Also, something on which associated things depend; the keystone of one's philosophy (unabridged)

Page 8 Equal but Unequal

Homonym: A word pronounced the same as another, but differing in meaning, whether spelled the same way or not.

1. A tabular register of days according to a system usually covering a year (abridged); A machine in which cloth, paper, or the like is smoothed, glazed by pressing between rotating cylinders (abridged)

2. One who predicts future events (abridged); dry (abridged)

3. Unsuccessful, useless (abridged); blood vessel (abridged)

4. To commend, glorify (abridged); to make raids for the sake of booty (abridged)

5. The dominion of one resembling a monarch (abridged); a line fastened to a bit by which a rider controls an animal (abridged)

6. To fasten by stitches (abridged); to plant seed (abridged)

7. To refer to (abridged); place or location (abridged)

8. Power or energy (abridged); a very little (abridged)

9. To draw or pull along behind (abridged); one of members of a foot (abridged)

10. Beautiful and popular girl (abridged); hollow and metallic device that vibrates and gives forth a ringing sound when struck (abridged)

93

GA1081

Page 9 Head for the Hills
headlong, head-on, headrest, headroom, headset, head start, headstone, headstrong, headway, heady

Page 10 Likes and Unlikes
Synonym—A word having the same or nearly the same meaning as another
Antonym—A word opposite in meaning to another
1. contract and expand 2. refuse and accept 3. overstatement and understatement 4. completion and failure 5. tough and tender 6. preceding and following 7. hindrance and assistance 8. fake and genuine 9. allow and forbid 10. shy and bold

Page 11 Add-Ons
Prefix—An affix attached to the beginning of a word
Suffix—An affix that occurs at the end of a word
1. before (prefix) 2. body of knowledge (suffix) 3. a separation into component parts (suffix) 4. a kind of written or spoken language (suffix) 5. half (prefix) 6. man (prefix) 7. sun (prefix) 8. one (prefix) 9. wood (prefix) 10. water (prefix)
  Possible answers:
  1. precede—come before
  2. paleontology—study of fossil remains
  3. analyze—to subject to scientific analysis
  4. dialogue—a conversation between two or more people
  5. semicircle—one half of a circle
  6. homogeneous—of the same or a similar kind or nature
  7. solarium—a room exposed to the sun
  8. unicorn—having one horn
  9. xylophone—a percussion instrument consisting of wooden bars, graduated in length to produce the musical scale
10. hydroelectric—production of electricity by waterpower

Page 12 Esoteric Cogitations
1. private eye 2. speaking one's mind (thoughts) 3. cowardly tramp 4. native 5. timely occurrence 6. stubborn ox 7. breakfast 8. hat 9. cab driver 10. free "eats" (food)

Page 13 Loop-the-Loop Puzzle

```
S E R F M B I B L E O
P H O N E T I C S W V
E R A D Z W R T U B A
L M O Z L D V B F T S
L N L N R P R E F I X
I P Q A O N U P I G R
N O U N N U I L X R Q
G M R T C N N P Y Z U
O O N O S I P L R E O
O T O N N G A A E M T
B E L Y R D Y L T I E
A F D M I U N S H O S
E R G S Y N O N Y M S
```

Pages 15-17 Look It Up (Answers here will vary.)
1. Mars planet: Ptolemy's theory; robots in space; space probes; tilt of the axis of Mars, diagram (Using *New Book of Knowledge*)
2. under musical instruments

94

GA1081

3. Socialism, econ. theory   Capitalism, theory
    Marx, Karl   Marx's analysis of
    Poverty, cures for   Poverty, cures for
    What are differences between   Trust, monopoly
   Communism, Socialism   regulation
    Women, role of
    Communism
       Civil war in China   Marx, Karl
       Communes   Nazism
       Econ. system   1 party system
       Education in China   Religion in China
       Fascism and Communism in Italy   SE Asia
       Hungary   Stalin and Russian Communist Party
       International relations   USSR
       Korean War   Differences between
       Lenin, Vladimir Ilich   Communism, Socialism

(All of the above from *Encyclopedia Americana*)

4. Look under *Cutlery.*

5. Under *Welfare* in *Compton's*, there's a cross reference to social legislation.

6. Under *Air Pollution* (*Colliers*)

7. Look under *Los Angeles Freeways.* (*Americana*)

8. Honeybee: Apidae, picture; see also Bee, animal navigation, orienting behavior (*Compton's*)

9. Aquinas   Positivism
   Heraclitus   Space and time
   Indian philosophy   Transcendence
   Infinity   Whitehead
   Judaism
   phenomenalism   (*Colliers*)
   Plato

10. archeology, art and architecture, cultural and social life, economic development, history, natural resources, people and population, religion, transportation. (*Americana*)

11. A few of books listed:
Early, Lawrence O. *Yanqui Politics and the Isthmian Canal.*
LaFeber, Walter. *The Panama Canal: The Crisis in Historical Perspective.*
McCullough, David. *The Path Between the Seas: The Creation of the Panama Canal.*
(*Americana*)

12. See also individual countries (*Americana*)

13. Alsop, Joseph. *FDR. 1882-1945: A Centenary Remembrance*
Bishop, Jim. *FDR's Last Year: April, 1944-April, 1945*
Dallek, Robert. *Franklin D. Roosevelt and American Foreign Policy*
(A few from *World Book*)

14. Look under *Roosevelt, Franklin D. Supreme Court.* (*Americana*)

15. Look under *Glenn, John Herschel, Jr.* (American Astro). (*Americana*)

16. Look under *Government, Law, Politics.* (*Colliers*)

17. ill or Ill

18. (paint.) also, just "ill" (*Colliers*)

19. General heading is in bold face. Subheading is indented and not in bold face.

20. Check under *Mural Painting.*

GA1081

Page 18 Animal Crackers (Used *Compton's* and *Americana*)

1. Elaphas Indicus or Loxodonta (African)	calf	herd
2. Meleagris gallopavo	poult	flock
3. cetasea	calf	school, pod
4. panthera leo	cub	pride
5. genera Vulpes	kit, pup, cub	skulk
6. sus scrofa	piglet	drove
7. ana tidae	duckling	team
8. Branta anatidae	gosling	gaggle
9. pisces (applied to all)	fingerling	school
10. odocoileus virginianus (white-tailed)	fawn	herd

Pages 19-20 Topics, Limited (Answers may vary because of use of different texts.)

1. *Colliers*
   Circus
      Acrobat on horseback
2. *Compton's*
   John F. Kennedy
      Assassination
         Dallas
      Church and State issue
      Cuban missile crisis and embargo
      Eisenhower
      Johnson
      Medals
      Nixon
      Peace Corps
      Profiles in Courage
      U.S. history
      Vietnamese War

3. *Compton's*
   Hang gliding
      Type of glider
      Air flight design
4. *Compton's*
   Alaska
   American Indians
   Bow drill
   Canada
      Newfoundland
      Northwest Territories
      Clothing
      Folktales
   Greenland
   Hunting customs
      seal
   North America
   Phys. classification
   Reindeer
   Shelter

Page 21 Claim to Fame

1. makes wigs 2. blacksmith 3. makes barrels, casks 4. one who drives a wagon 5. makes hats 6. cuts fabrics for garments 7. tinsmith 8. makes utensils, jewelry out of copper 9. makes glassware 10. makes horseshoes and shoes horses. Occupations done today: 1,3,5,6,7,8,9,10.

Pages 22-23 Happy Holidays

1. Yes. Throughout U.S. and in cities where there are many Polish Americans. There are parades and festivities.
2. Started in France with playing tricks. A person who was fooled, called a poisson d'avril (fish of April). Story is that in April the fish are young and easily caught.
3. To observe the anniversary of the day, June 14, 1777, when Congress adopted the Stars and Stripes as the national flag of the U.S. Flags are on display. June 14

GA1081

4. Memorial Day—Honors all Americans who died in Civil War and the wars following. Armistice Day was when WWI ended. In the U.S., now called Veterans' Day and honors all men and women who served in nation's armed forces.

5. Some say for St. Valentine. He was thrown into jail by the Romans because he wouldn't worship their gods. He loved children and while he was in jail, children threw messages to him through the window of jail cell.

6. All Saints' Day or All Hallows' Day to honor the saints, who had no day of their own.

7. To honor working people. Peter McGuire, a carpenter.

8. The time when the sun crosses the plane of the earth's equator, making night and day of approximate equal length all over the earth. March 21.

9. Not a real national holiday, as far as parades and other celebrations are concerned. It is observed, though, on February 2 when the groundhog crawls out of his den, and if he sees his shadow, it means 6 more weeks of winter. If the animal doesn't see his shadow, then spring will be soon.

10. October 10 is when Capt. Cook discovered Hawaii.

Page 26 Cryptogram

1. people 2. places 3. events 4. animals 5. plants 6. things 7. cross references 8. discoveries 9. inventions 10. see also references 11. history 12. biography 13. bibliography 14. countries 15. maps 16. dates 17. economics 18. geography 19. photographs 20. charts

Pages 29-32 The Cards Will Tell

1. *Heart of Darkness, Typhoon* (Answers will vary.)

2. Holidays—Jews   See also
   See   Anniversaries
     Fasts and Feasts (Judaism)   Arbor Day
                           Christmas
  (Answers will vary.)   Fasts and Feasts
                           Fourth of July

3. See also: Amusements, Ball games, Cards, Dancing, Educational games, Group games, Indoor games (Answers will vary.)

4. Look under *China*.

5. Look under *Gardner, Erle Stanley*.

6. (Answers will vary.) Bates, Rich. *The Gentleman from Ohio*

7. (Nos. 7,8,9,10,11 Answers will vary.)

History	Navy
In Literature	Nobility
Laws	Orators
Maps	Politics
Municipal Government	Provinces
Nationalism and Religion	Social Life, Customs

8. None

9. History and Criticism, U.S. and Criticism, Musicians, Music England, U.S.

10. Weren't any in my library.

11. Condon, Edward, *Final Report of Scientific Study of UFOs*
Jacobs, David Michael. *The UFO Controversy in America*
Klass, Philip J. *UFOs Explained*
Lore, Gordon. *Mysteries of the Skies*
Menzel, Donald. *The World of Flying Saucers*

GA1081

12. Nonfiction book, published 1964, 250 pages, illus. map
13. Fiction, alphabetical on shelf, according to last name of author, Hersey
14. Title card
15. Author card, along the 658 shelf
16. Look under *Teenage* or *Adolescence*.
17. Subject
18. (Answer will vary.)

Vision
  See also
    After images
    Artificial vision
    Color vision
    Eye

Optical illusions
Optics
Visual perception

19. Subject
20. Reference section

Page 34 A Complete Job
The Complete Adventures of the Borrowers
Complete Beginners' Guide to Bowling
The Complete Book of Cheerleading
Complete Book of the Dance
Complete Book of Dragons
Complete Book of Fairy Tales and Stories
Complete Book of Horses
Complete Book of Indian Crafts and Lore
The Complete Book of Kite Making
The Complete Book of Photography

Page 34 ABC's of a Book
A certain shepherd; Did you carry the clay today, Charley?
Happy little family; A pocketful of cricket; A schoolhouse in the woods

Page 36 Paper Chase for Authors
1. Joan Nixon 2. Robert C. O'Brien 3. Jim Kjelgaard 4. Mary Stolz 5. Lee Wyndham 6. Marjorie Sharmat 7. Jean Lee Latham 8. Mina Lewiton 9. Richard Peck 10. Henry Winterfield 11. Vivian L. Thompson 12. Marguerite Henry 13. Iris Noble 14. David Weingast 15. Flora Seymour 16. Sterling North 17. Albert Payson Terhune 18. William MacKeller 19. Eloise Jarvis McGraw 20. Augusta Stevens

Page 37 Paper Chase for Titles
1. *Dinky Hocker Shoots Smack* 2. *Shane* 3. *Ben and Me* 4. *Danger Beats the Drum* 5. *Johnny Tremaine* 6. *The Changeling* 7. *A Wind Through the Door* 8. *Encyclopedia Brown* 9. *The Secret of the Elms* 10. *The Red Room Riddle*
(Answers in the Paper Chase—Authors and Titles—will undoubtedly vary, although the selection of names was made, based on well-known authors and their works, who would be represented in a school library.)

GA1081

The crossword solution reads:

1. CARDS
2. COPYRIGHT
3. REF
4. STORY
5. DEWEY
6. CLASS
7. TITLE
8. AUTHOR
9. LASTNAME
10. ALSO
11. DRAWERS
12. SUBJECT
13. BIOGRAPHY

Pages 40-42 A Guide for All

1. See *Solar energy* 2. Look under *SWAT* 3. "Four Vital Questions About Your Skin" *House and Garden* 147:36+ Ap '75 4. under *Pennsylvania* 5. See also *Rock concerts*; *Paul Simon* 6. Porn rock: "The Controversy Rolls On. R. Rothenstein 45:69-70+ Mar '86 7. Mech Illus: "Snowmobiles That Go Like the Wind." S. James. 74:48+ S '78 8. See *Rock groups* 9. Robert Edwin Lee and Jerome Lawrence 10. Asset-backed financing; Banks and banking; Bonds; Bonds, government; Default; Federal Reserve System (U.S.) 11. Figure Skating. MacLean's, 101 Sp. Issue 24-6+ F '88, Lighting up the Late Shift, Sports Illus. 68:38-40+ Ja 18 '88 Thomas recaptures title, eyes Olympic skating win, D. Thomas Jet 73:52 Ja 25 '88

12. "Incredible Saga of a One-Legged Duck" 13. "Assertion of Dolphin Rights Fails in Court—C. Holden. Sci 199:37 Ja 6 '78

"Do Dolphins Have Legal Rights" O. Hoyt. Encore 7:38 Ap 17 '78

14. R.T. Bakker

15. Camp Counsel should be camp counsel. M.L. Northway. Camping Mag 46:12+ F '74

    Camp staff training; agency coop creates new program. L Weiss. Camp Mag 46:9+ Ap '74

16. Shop Talk. A.J. Hand. Pop Sci 229:20 Ag '86

17. AIDS, Airports, Art Trade, Bridges, Civil Rights, Indians

18. End of the Glorious Ordeal. R. Fimrite. Sport Illus 40:20-3

GA1081

19. Craig, Rogers   Piniella, Lou
    Herzog, Whitey   Rose, Pete
    Howser, Dick   Stengl, Casey
    Johnson, Davey   Williams, Dick
20. If you look under *Women*, you'll find authors, bartenders, biologists, clergy, cooks, executives, insurance agents, lawyers, paralegals, physicians, etc.

Pages 43-44 Lost Articles
1. *Children's Guide*—Subjects listed in alphabetical order.
   Reader's Guide—Authors, subjects, titles, alphabetical order. See references and see also. Also book, dance, movie, record, radio program, TV program, video disc, and tape reviews. Symbols are different because magazines are.
2. Christmas Sneaker. J.H. Corwin. Ebony, Jr. Dec. '84 P. 37.
   Gifts with Meaning. L. Graeber. Young Miss. Dec. '84 P. 26.
3. Humpty Dumpty Dec. '84 P. 9-11
4. Photographer. Nat Wildlife Oct.-Nov. '84 P. 40-45.
5. 3-2-1 Contact Sept. '83 P.14
6. Feb. '85 P. 14-17
7. Sci World Oct. 19 '84 P. 10 +
8. Enter Nov. '84 P. 32-35
9. Sci World Sept. 20 '85 P. 12-15
10. A. Burkitt Feb.-Mar. '85 P. 30-31
11. A Bedtime Story: All About Sleep. Choices Oct. '86 P. 24-25
12. Crocodile Rescue. Owl Apr '84 P. 26-29
13. A Monster from the Briny Deep. J. Kotsilibar-Davis. Sci Dig 94:88 Mar '86
    Crocodiles, Fossil "Weird Crocodile" discovered
    by Louis L. Jacobs and Z. Kaufulu Sci News 129:343 May 31, 1986
14. "Why I Believe That Women Must Exercise Their Political Clout"
15. See also phobias; Toddler Fears. J. Gibson. Parents 59:166 N '84

Pages 45-46 Between the Lines

1. "Hideout" by Lois Lenski
2. "The Ballad of Hagensack" by Wallace Irwin
3. "Wynken, Blynken, and Nod" by Eugene Field
4. "My Shadow" by Robert Louis Stevenson
5. "Bed in Summer" by Robert Louis Stevenson
6. "The Owl and the Pussycat" by Edward Lear
7. "Buckingham Palace" by A.A. Milne
8. "Song of Hiawatha" by Henry Wadsworth Longfellow
9. "A Coughdrop Lies in My Doghouse" by K.J. Kennedy
10. L. Hughes
11. "Taught Me Purple" by S.T. Hunt
12. "In Schooldays," "Snowbound," "Skipper Ireson's Ride"
13. It gives first line of poetry. *RG* does not.
14. He wrote limericks. "Nonsense Alphabet," "Calico Pie," "The Duck and the Kangaroo," "The Jumblies," "The Quangle Wangle's Hat," "The Cummerbund."

Page 47 Square Roots
title, issue, **magazine**, writer, subject, pages

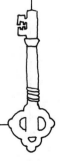

     GA1081

Page 49-50 To a Great Degree
1. 1931 Berline de Voyage Royall (8.1 million)
2. Protestant Cathedral of Ulm, Germany
3. North: Dr. Frederick Albert Cook and Rear Adm. Robert Edwin Peary. South: 193 men (crew) of the Resolution under Capt. James Cook
4. 1200 miles (Portugal) won by Emir
5. Mona Lisa
6. $6000 paid by Baron Schroder to Sanders of St. Albans
7. Looked under *Cook, Frederick Albert Dr.*
   Looked under *Peary, Robert Edwin.* There were no "see" references, using *Colliers.*
8. *The People's Almanac;* painters
9. Used *Colliers:* Adam and Eve   No. American
   Coral root   rattlesnake plantain
   grass pink   seed
   Hawaii   tree orchid
   Holy Ghost flower
   lady's slipper
   lady's tresses
10. Any almanac of 1988 that records world events for 1987. Encyclopedia yearbook would also have something similar.

Pages 51-52 Follow the Trail
1. *Doubleday:* The Universe, Our Planet, Countries of the World, History of the World, World of Animals, World of Plants, World of Science and Technology, World of Art and Entertainment, World of Sports, World of Transportation and Communication, World of Religion, Miscellany.
   Lincoln has basically the same, except gives the headings different titles. The *New Lincoln* composed of 3 volumes, as opposed to *Doubleday's* only one volume. The *Lincoln* is arranged in 12 broad topical sections, called departments, covering roughly the same areas as *Doubleday.*
2. For example, *Doubleday's* World of Transportation and Communication becomes Transportation and Inventions in *Lincoln;* information is also more extensive.
1. India
2. Napoleonic (*Doubleday*)
3. 300 meter freestyle swim; 4000 meter cross country run; 5000 meter equestrian steeplechase; epee fencing; pistol target 25 meters shooting
4. Scrambling (motorcross), trials, grasstrack racing
5. Czech athlete and runner, 18 world records and Olympic titles
6. Rock jazz West Indies (Jamaica, specifically)
7. Doric, Ionic, Corinthian
8. David Brewer
9. One part of optic nerve head does not contain any nerve endings. When you turn your head in certain direction, there's no vision.
10. 90,000-140,000
11. Montezuma cypress
12. Original people of Australia
13. Arctic
14. Pacific
15. Deep canyon cut into the continental shelf, offshore from mouth of river.
16. 4.6 billion years
17. Cetus, Sculptor, Aquarius

GA1081

18. Delphinus, Pegasus, Pisces
19. 2 weeks
20. Lieut. Gen. 5th and 6th Chinese armies in Burma. After fall of Burma, placed in command of American forces in China. In 1945, in command of 10th Army, Pacific Theater.

Page 53 What's My Name?

1. Mary Jane Canary
2. Duke of Wellington
3. James Madison
4. Andrew Jackson
5. General George Patton, Jr.
6. Thomas Jefferson
7. William F. Cody
8. William H. Harrison
9. General Zachary Taylor
10. General Ulysses S. Grant

11. *New Book of Knowledge*
    Calamity Jane
    American Frontier Personality
    Colliers
       Old Hickory
       See Andrew Jackson

    Compton's
    Buffalo Bill
       U.S. Frontiersman
       frontier

       marksmanship
       Western
       Wild West Show
          Hickok
          Oakley

Pages 54-55 Dig for Clues

1. Arizona 2. Powhatan 3. octopus 4. Alaska 5. Paderewski (Ignace) 6. Atlas 7. Olympia, a plain in ancient Elis, Greece 8. California 9. Benjamin Franklin 10. John Rolfe 11. 56 12. Spanish American 13. *Monitor* 14. First child of English parents to be born in America August 18, 1587 15. Denver 16. New Orleans 17. "God Save the King" 18. Blown up in Havana Harbor February 15, 1898. U.S. went to war with Spain. 19. Because he collaborated with the Nazis in WWII. A person who betrays his own country by aiding an invading enemy. 20. From Dawson Creek, British Columbia to Fairbanks, Alaska 21. Traveler 22. Goldenrod 23. Young women of Portsmouth, New Hampshire, for Captain John Paul Jones 24. Separates the waters draining into the Atlantic Ocean from those draining into the Pacific. 25. yes

Page 56 Behind the Scenes

1. Franklin Delano Roosevelt
2. Franklin Delano Roosevelt
3. Woodrow Wilson
4. Andrew Johnson
5. Thomas Jefferson
6. James Madison
7. Woodrow Wilson
8. James Madison
9. Andrew Johnson
10. Abraham Lincoln

Page 57 Strictly Speaking

1. Erebus
2. V.P. Bush
3. Jan. 3, 1981 (*Reader's Digest Almanac*)
4. Scale of numbers representing wind force in open ground
5. Clean Water Act and Emergency Aid for Homeless (Answers may vary.)
6. Joe Rosenthal
7. Dallas Opera, Fort Worth Opera, Houston Opera
8. Citibank, N.Y.
9. Laurent Fabius

10. 1111 Broad Locust Bldg., Philadelphia, PA 19102; 4900 members
11. John Stennis
12. We Dare Defend Our Rights
13. *Mary Celeste*
14. $200,000
15. North Capital at H Streets NW, Washington, D.C. 20401

Page 58 Strays
  1. Legal holiday
  2. 17
  3. Sagebrush
  4. 1801
  5. Sept. 8-11, 1920
  6. Good evening
  7. In Norse tales. Wolfskin shirt used by which man becomes wolf for 9 days out of 10.
  8. When a death occurs in a family, someone must go to the hives to tell the bees.
  9. Barbers once practiced bleeding and leeching. The red is for the blood; the white, bandages.
 10. Yes, faithful love

Pages 58-59 Famous Utterances
  1. Franklin D. Roosevelt
  2. William Prescott
  3. Commander James Lawrence
  4. John Paul Jones
  5. Will Rogers
  6. Theodore Roosevelt
  7. Daniel Webster
  8. Benjamin Franklin

Pages 60-61 All of a Heap
  1. Tigran Petrosian
  2. The Cullinan
  3. John George Diefenbaker, Conservative
  4. 18,340
  5. 8 hours 6 minutes, Chicago White Sox vs. Milwaukee Brewers May 9, 1984
  6. Austin, Texas
  7. Dam
  8. Henry Aaron
  9. No one
 10. Jaipur, India
 11. O'Hare
 12. clay relief of leopards, southern Anatolia, Turkey 6200 B.C.
 13. 185 Salisbury Street, Worcester, MA
 14. 1556 in Shensi, China; over 800,000 killed
 15. 755
 16. Captain and Tenille. "Love Will Keep Us Together"
 17. 2193.167 mph
 18. Russia
 19. $11.9 million. *The Gospel Book of Henry the Lion, Duke of Saxony*
 20. Salt Lake City, Utah
 21. Montana
 22. See currency (Answer may vary.)
 23. Congress, United States
 24. 301 Massachusetts Avenue, Symphony Hall, Boston, MA 02115

GA1081

25. Look under *Luge* or *Olympic Games*.

Page 62 Mix and Match
1. 2,3,4,8
2. 6
3. 2,3,7
4. 1

Page 63 The Best of All
1. Shut

C	L	O	S	E
22	18	10	8	21

2. Opposite of out

I	N
3	4

3. Something to eat

F	O	O	D
14	23	16	25

4. Labor

W	O	R	K
15	13	20	12

5. Lady's garment

D	R	E	S	S
19	24	6	7	26

6. Hunter's instrument

G	U	N
1	2	5

7. Steal

R	O	B
17	11	9

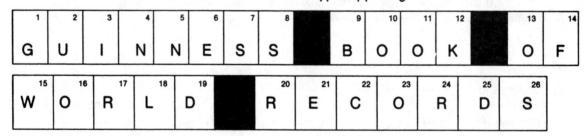

1	2	3	4	5	6	7	8		9	10	11	12		13	14
G	U	I	N	N	E	S	S		B	O	O	K		O	F

15	16	17	18	19		20	21	22	23	24	25	26
W	O	R	L	D		R	E	C	O	R	D	S

Pages 68-69 Here and There
1. Eastern part of Panama. That part of the isthmus between the Gulf of Darien on the East coast and the Gulf of San Miguel on the West coast.
2. The quarter section of Antarctic continent between Greenwich meridian and 90° East.
3. Yes. Northeast Illinois, 17 miles west of Chicago
4. Yes. Santa Rosa is in western California, trade center of Sonoma Valley, north of San Francisco. Santa Rosa, Florida, is on the Gulf of Mexico, east of Pensacola Naval Station, and is south of the city of Pensacola.

GA1081

5. Town northeast of West Virginia
6. Cape on northwest coast Jamaica
7. Louis Gentil
8. Bernalillo
9. Pennsylvania
10. Louisiana
11. *Webster's*—county in Illinois
   Lippincott—county Northwest Illinois. Bounded Northwest by Mississippi River; drained by Rock River and Rock and Elkhorn Creeks. Agriculture (livestock, corn, wheat, oats, hay, truck, poultry) limestone quarries. Processing of farm and dairy products; manufacturing machinery; home applicances; metal and wire products; hardware; gas engines; petroleum products. Includes natural wildlife refuge. *Lippincott* gives many more details.
12. Bighorn River, S. Montana
13. 1792, *Lippincott* gives more details about cities, products, history of state
14. *World Book*: Kentucky—See Boone, Daniel; Indian Wars; Kentucky and Virginia Resolutions; Westward Movement
15. *Webster's*—7,071,639 (1980 census)
   Lippincott—7,891,957 (1950 census)
   Encyclopedia (*Americana*)—7,071,639 (1980 census)
   World Almanac (1988)—,071,639
   Would use the figure with the most recent census, 1980.

Page 70 A Difference of Opinion
They both include pronunciation, location, area, population, geographical and physical description and economic and historical information. Both have cross references. However, *Lippincott* gives much more information about each place. It also has more entries (130,000) than *Webster* (48,000). *Webster* is compact; *Lippincott* is bulky to handle.

Pages 71-72 Trace the Place
I. It would give more feature sidelights of the festival, along with pictures. Look up *Spain*.

Changing Face of Old Spain
Included—Barcelona, Pamplona, Segovia, Seville,
Toledo, Valencia 291-339 Mar 1965
II. Craftsmen pound out horseshoes, dip candles, weave rugs, fashion tinware, weave baskets, make brooms.

Kutztown, Pa.
Penn. Dutch Folk Festival by Maynard Owen
Williams
503-516 Oct. 1952
III. *Book of Knowledge* (as one)
   Pennsylvania Dutch
      folk art

Page 73 True/False
1. T 2. F 3. F 4. F 5. T 6. F 7. T 8. T 9. T 10. F 11. T 12. F 13. F 14. T

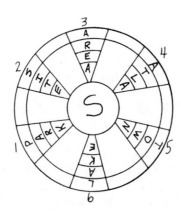

Pages 76-77 People Pleasers

1. *Who's Who*. Gives a brief sketch of who the person is and what he has done.

2. *Dictionary of American Biography* was far more extensive compared to the listing in the back of the dictionary and in the collective biography *Something About the Author. Compton's*, for example, had a good account, but still did not compare to that of the *DAB*.
    Compton's
        Alcott, Louisa May
            Children's reading
            Concord, Mass.

3. *Dictionary of American Biography* still the most extensive. *Americana* contains less details, but stimulates one to find out more.
    The account in the *Lincoln* is sketchy.
    The card catalog (Answers will vary.):
            Barton, Clara
                Red Cross
                Life of Clara Barton by William Eleazar Barton

4. *Who's Who in America*

5. *Encyclopedia Americana* (probably in other encyclopedias)

6. *DAB* is much more detailed.
    The card catalog (Answers will vary.):

Roosevelt, Theodore	Muscle Shoals
See Conservation	Panama Canal
Far East	Progressive Party
Forest service	Root, Elihu
Hague conferences	Taft, Wm. Robt.
History of presidency	Travels
McKinley	White House
Miners' strike	
Monroe Doctrine	

7. Rev. Charles Lutwidge Dodgson. *Alice in Wonderland*. He wrote a lot of books of mathematics under his real name, Dodgson, and probably wanted to keep his children's work separate and distinct under a pseudonym.

8. Nonfiction re-creates an actual life, just as it was. In a fictional biography the author, many times, invents characters and conversations.

9. Title card and author card

10. Alphabetically, according to author's last name

Page 78 Ladies, First
1. Grace A. Goodhue 2. Abigail Smith 3. Sarah Childress 4. Margaret Mackall Smith

GA1081

5. Mary Ann Todd 6. Martha Wayles 7. Julia Dent 8. Frances Folsom 9. Lucretia Rudolph 10. Ida Saxton 11. James Buchanan was a bachelor. 12. Helen Herron 13. Dolley Payne 14. Rachel Donelson Robards 15. Alice Hathaway Lee and Edith Kermit Carow 16. Hannah Hoes 17. Elizabeth Kortright 18. Louisa Catherine Johnson 19. Eliza McCardle 20. Anna Tuthill Symmes

Pages 79-80 First with the Most
1. inventor, fountain pen 2. inventor, Yale lock 3. engineer, designer Brooklyn Bridge 4. Colonial poet, first book of poems by an English woman in America 5. dentist, first to practice in U.S. 6. merchant, founder Wanamaker Dept. Store 7. writer, juvenile fiction, originated Tom Swift, Bobbsey Twins series 8. physician, first woman doctor of modern times 9. leader of mob which precipitated Boston Massacre 10. circus performer, General Tom Thumb 11. poet and short story writer, father of modern detective story 12. Nellie Bly. She went around the world in less than the 80 days of Jules Verne's Phineas Fogg: 72 days, 6 hours and 11 minutes 13. Molly Pitcher. She carried water for the soldiers during the Battle of Monmouth in Revolutionary War. 14. Light Horse Harry Lee, father of Robert E. Lee 15. Constitutional Union Party, 1860; John Bell of Tennessee

Pages 81-82 Catch a Rising Star
1. entertainer 2. marine explorer, film producer, writer 3. opera producer 4. actress 5. Retired Air Force officer, test pilot 6. Secretary of Housing and Urban Development (HUD) 7. actress 8. Secretary of State 9. comedian, writer 10. painter 11. composer 12. Secretary of Army 13. 1961-1965 14. World Press Rev; June, '87, P. 53, "Cousteau's Plea for the Mediterranean" 16. Edna Rae Gillooly 17. "Billy the Kid," "Appalachian Spring" 20. Popular Mechanics. 164:90-2 21. "Chuck Yeager Sees Changes in the Air"

Pages 83-84 Civil Servants
1. Secretary of State, Lincoln 2. Speaker of H.R., Wilson; Ill., Ia., Neb., Ca. 3. V.P. McKinley 4. V.P. Theodore Roosevelt 5. Secretary Treasurer, Lincoln 6. Chief Justice, Washington 7. Chief Justice, John Adams 8. Secretary Treasurer, Washington 9. Chief Justice, Washington 10. Governor of Wisconsin, 11. Attorney General, Eisenhower; Secretary of State, Nixon 12. Secretary of Labor, Nixon; Secretary of State, Reagan 13. V.P. Nixon; President, 1974-1977 14. Secretary of Defense, Nixon 16. Alaska; purchased by Secretary of State Seward and denounced as a waste of money.

Page 85 Thumbnail Sketches
1. physicist, inventor, founder Polaroid Company, invented Polaroid camera 2. physician, scientist; developed vaccine for polio 3. physicist, educator; discoverer radiation belts around Earth 4. research physicist, Nobel Prize Chemistry, 1985 5. mathematician, educator, researcher, Nobel Prize Chemistry, 1985 6. consumer advocate, lawyer, author; *Unsafe at Any Speed* 7. composer; 800 8. author, *Texas* 9. radio, TV news correspondent 10. philosopher, author 11. *Rolling Stone*. Nov. 5-Dec. 10, 1987; P. 87 +; J. Alter 12. *50 Plus*. "It's Still Speed Ahead for Ralph Nader"; 24-7. 13. *Rolling Stone*

Page 86 Rebus Twister
CET + DOLL + EYE - DYE + CLOCK - LOCKET + T + FIVE - F = collective
BI + O + GRAPH + YOU - OU = biography

GA1081

Pages 87-90 Find the Resource

1. Unabridged dictionary
2. Unabridged dictionary
3. Encyclopedia
4. *Reader's Guide to Periodical Literature*
5. Vertical file
6. *Guinness Book of World Records*
7. Vertical file
8. Encyclopedia
9. Card catalog
10. Card catalog
11. Encyclopedia
12. Vertical file
13. Encyclopedia. Unabridged dicitonary might help, too.
14. *Guinness Book of World Records*
15. See vertical file
16. Card catalog
17. Abridged dictionary, also unabridged
18. Abridged dictionary, also unabridged
19. Card catalog
20. Encyclopedia, also card catalog
21. *Reader's Guide to Periodical Literature*
22. Abridged dictionary, also unabridged dictionary
23. Unabridged dictionary
24. *Columbia Lippincott Gazeteer of the World*, also unabridged dictionary
25. *Reader's Guide to Periodical Literature*
26. Unabridged dictionary
27. Card catalog
28. *Guinness Book of World Records*
29. *Lincoln Library of Essential Information*
30. Card catalog will have books. Encyclopedia could give brief description.
31. Abridged and unabridged dictionaries
32. Card catalog
33. Encyclopedia
34. Vertical file
35. *Columbia Lippincott Gazeteer of the World*, also encyclopedia
36. *Lincoln Library of Essential Information*, also encyclopedia
37. *Columbia Lippincott Gazeteer of the World*
38. *Children's Magazine Guide*
39. *Children's Magazine Guide*
40. *Index to Poetry for Children and Young People*
41. *Columbia Lippincott Gazeteer of the World*
42. *Columbia Lippincott Gazeteer of the World*
43. *Lincoln Library of Essential Information*
44. *Lincoln Library of Essential Information*, also encyclopedia
45. Either in the abridged or unabridged dictionary
46. *Reader's Guide to Periodical Literature*
47. Vertical file
48. Encyclopedia
49. *World Almanac* (or any almanac that would answer the question)
50. Card catalog

108

GA1081